Praise for *The Complexity Crisis*

"The book was clear and to the point. It deals with an important topic and readers will reap great benefits from it."

—Ram Charan, consultant and author of
Execution—The Art of Getting Things Done

"John Mariotti could not have chosen a subject that is more relevant to today's business world. Many who read his book will think Mariotti somehow got an inside peek at their business—his observations and recommendations in *The Complexity Crisis* are so on point with the challenges that we face in business today."

—Gary Baughman, CEO of Petmate Corporation
and former CEO of Fisher-Price

"I recommend *The Complexity Crisis* to any C-level executive who is serious about competing and improving the sustainability of their business in an ever changing global marketplace."

—Peter Strople, chairman and CEO, The Zero2 Companies,
former director DELL Computer Corporation, and former
director of GRiD Systems Corp. (Inventor of the
Modern Clamshell Laptop Computer)

"If your costs are up and profits down, you should devour John Mariotti's terrific book on 'Complexity'!"

—Jack C. Shewmaker, executive consultant, retired president and
vice chairman, Wal-Mart Stores, Inc.

"Complexity comes from not understanding your customers' needs. This has resulted in companies drowning their customers in proliferated products and services. John Mariotti delivers a powerful message in this era of mass customization.

—Roy Marsten, chief scientist,
Emcien Corporation

"In *The Complexity Crisis*, John Mariotti is holding up a very big mirror to an impending calamity."

—Daniel Moneypenny, president and
chief creative officer, Emaginit

"It is not possible to read *The Complexity Crisis* without thinking very differently about one's industry and business model. This is a must read for any executive seriously interested in improving their organization's performance and profitability."

—Robert J. Herson, president,
Executive Focus International, Inc.

"*The Complexity Crisis* provides new and provocative insights into a major problem facing modern corporations. Mariotti is *the* expert on Complexity and the solutions he offers are the best I've seen."

—James B. Swartz, author, *Seeing David in
the Stone* and *The Hunters and the Hunt*

"If I were still running a business or a government organization, *The Complexity Crisis* would be required reading for all of my executives and managers. John Mariotti builds a compelling case on how being too complex is drowning employees, slowing growth, and degrading profit. Most importantly, he provides a practical approach on how to fix the problem—in a quick and truly rewarding read."

—Vice Admiral Ed Straw, U.S. Navy (retired),
former director, Defense Logistics Agency,
and former president, Global Operations,
The Estee Lauder Companies

"Any book about what to do about the "Complexity Crisis" is worth reading. Complexity is the enemy of effective marketing. Simplicity is the holy grail."

—Jack Trout, consultant and noted author of
several bestsellers, including *Positioning—
The Battle for your Mind* and *The New Positioning*

"John Mariotti is making a call for everyone's attention to this reality, and we'd better pay attention to his call and make the world change and return to simplicity."

—Carlos Villa, publisher, Tiempe de Mercadeo,
Medellin, Colombia

"I thoroughly enjoyed *The Complexity Crisis.* I applaud John for not only pointing out what complexity is, but also how to measure it and how to 'lose it.' I also liked how he doesn't let companies off the hook and allow themselves to be victims."

—Rich Daugherty, executive vice president,
Operations, Petmate Corporation

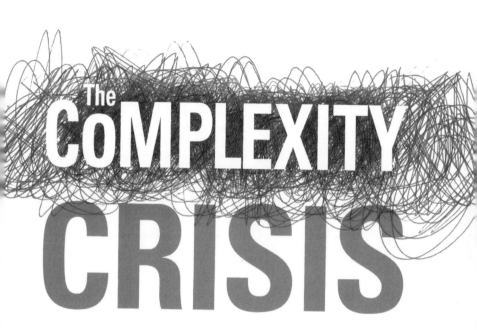

The CoMPLEXITY CRISIS

WHY TOO MANY PRODUCTS, MARKETS, AND CUSTOMERS ARE CRIPPLING YOUR COMPANY—

AND WHAT TO DO ABOUT IT

JOHN L. MARIOTTI

PLATINUM PRESS®

AVON, MASSACHUSETTS

The Platinum Press® is a registered trademark of F+W Publications, Inc.

Published by Adams Media, an F+W Publications Company
57 Littlefield Street
Avon, MA 02322
www.adamsmedia.com

ISBN-10: 1-59869-214-3
ISBN-13: 978-1-59869-214-3

Printed in the United States of America.
J I H G F E D C B A

Library of Congress Cataloging-in-Publication Data
Mariotti, John L.
The complexity crisis / John L. Mariotti.
p. cm.
Includes bibliographical references.
ISBN-13: 978-1-59869-214-3 (hardcover)
ISBN-10: 1-59869-214-3 (hardcover)
1. Organizational effectiveness. 2. Process control.
3. Cost control. 4. Quality control. I. Title.
HD58.9.M374 2007
338.501—dc22   2007015888

This publication is designed to provide accurate and authoritative information with
regard to the subject matter covered. It is sold with the understanding that the publisher is not engaged in rendering legal, accounting, or other professional advice. If
legal advice or other expert assistance is required, the services of a competent professional person should be sought.
—From a *Declaration of Principles* jointly adopted by a Committee of the American
Bar Association and a Committee of Publishers and Associations

Many of the designations used by manufacturers and sellers to distinguish their product are claimed as trademarks. Where those designations appear in this book and
Adams Media was aware of a trademark claim, the designations have been printed
with initial capital letters.

This book is available at quantity discounts for bulk purchases.
For information, please call 1-800-289-0963.

CONTENTS

Contents

PART THREE—The Solutions

INTRODUCTION

"Talent hits a target no one else can hit; genius hits a target no one else can see."
—Arthur Schopenhauer, nineteenth-century German philosopher

Companies all over the world are struggling with a crisis. Most troubling of all is that most of these companies don't realize that it is a crisis of their own making. Nor do most of them understand what to do about it. They are starting to realize that this crisis—the Complexity Crisis—is crippling them, destroying their profits, and draining their resources.

The actions that have created the Complexity Crisis are usually taken with the best of intentions. In the quest for high growth in low/no-growth markets, companies have proliferated nearly everything: products, customers, markets, suppliers, facilities, locations, etc. Some of the time, the proliferation actually does lead to top-line revenue growth, but as the top line goes up, the bottom line—profit—doesn't. In many cases, the bottom line actually goes down dramatically.

The Complexity Crisis is worsened by the fact that none of today's pervasive accounting systems identify complexity costs until it is too late. By then, the company is "in crisis" and it doesn't understand exactly why. None of the current measurement systems reveal what is happening until the end of accounting periods, when the negative bottom-line impact is evident. The causes, however, are still obscured, buried in variances, special charges, increased overhead, and more "catch-all" categories.

Everyone I tell about unrecognized complexity has the same reaction: Their eyes widen slightly and they say, "Of course, that's right. It *is* a problem!" After a moment of thought, they add, "It's a big problem. Why hasn't anyone exposed this before?" Now someone has.

Complexity—It's Everywhere!

The airline industry is a poster child of complexity, with its yield-based pricing policies, proliferation of routes, fare/class structures, aircraft variations, and more. Just watch the keystrokes a counterperson for an airline must make to do a simple flight change. Or imagine if the airline had to post a seat map of the plane for customers to see the many different fares and how widely they vary. Business travelers, flying on short notice, might be sitting next to leisure travelers who shopped and booked well in advance, and paying anywhere from two to five times the fare for the same trip. Only companies like Southwest and its emulators have broken the code on this one. The major airlines are just figuring it out, which they will need to do if they want to survive.

Everyone realizes that U.S. automakers Ford and GM are in crisis. Complexity is at the root of their troubles, too: too many brands, too many models, too many dealers, too many plants, too many union work restrictions, and on and on. DaimlerChrysler is not immune to the Complexity Crisis either. Consider Mercedes-Benz, as it clings desperately to its luxury-market position. BMW and Lexus rival it in prestige. Audi, Acura, Infiniti, and Cadillac are gaining. New Korean rivals are encroaching.

Are M-B's recent woes a simple case of competition? No. Part of Mercedes' problems is directly related to self-induced complexity. Since Daimler's acquisition of Chrysler, its complexity is much greater. Mercedes-Benz's problems—lapses in quality, deteriorating profits, and continued service issues—are all rooted in self-inflicted complexity. The number of Mercedes models sold in the United States in 1995 was only twenty, up from six or seven at its U.S. entry in 1957. It has now proliferated to forty-five models, more than doubling in ten years. The number of models grows each year—as does the complexity Mercedes-Benz must manage.

That doesn't even count Chrysler models that use partial Mercedes platforms (Crossfire, 300C, etc.), requiring collaborative engineering support. Perhaps it is no surprise that Mercedes has struggled. The Complexity Crisis is an unrecognized cause of many such problems, and Mercedes has no special exemption.

Make no mistake, companies need new products to compete, but how many, and how they are developed, introduced, and managed, makes a huge difference in the amount of complexity added. The same goes for entering new markets, opening new facilities, and so forth. Only when a company realizes its problems are complexity driven and "takes a breather" to consolidate, simplify, and measure/manage the complexity, do the problems start to shrink away. Until then, they just keep growing.

The Problem: Where Have All the Profits Gone?

Businesses must compete in more complex global markets than ever before. Most companies are seeking double-digit growth in markets growing at low-single-digit rates—or not growing at all. This quest for growth has led to runaway complexity caused by the proliferation of products, customers, markets, suppliers, services, locations, and more. All of these add costs, which go untracked by even the best of modern accounting systems. Complexity also fragments management focus, wastes time and money, and ultimately reduces shareholder value. The problems grow, but they remain under the radar of management attention. Complexity is arguably the most insidious, hidden profit drain in today's business world.

The Challenge: What Can You Do About It?

First, you need to recognize that rampant proliferation adds to costs in a manner that goes untracked. Then track it down. Where it adds value, alter processes to capitalize on it. Where it doesn't (which is most places), stop it. Reduce or eliminate it, and institute safeguards—systems and metrics—to prevent its unnoticed return. Most of all, find quick, easy ways to describe this complexity so it is recognized as a potential profit drain, and managed like the critical business consideration it has become.

The Premise: What Gets Measured, Gets Managed

It is easy to get fat in good times. A few too many people, a few too many customers, a few too many products, and a few too many facilities—the volume of good times covers a multitude of sins.

One part of the problem is that people feel the need to create new products, processes, facilities, and systems, *but no one is designated to kill off the old obsolete or unproductive ones!* Product proliferation costs a fortune, but no accounting system captures the cost of extra part numbers, bills of materials, standards, training, and shorter runs/smaller purchases. Customers that cost more to keep than to lose hang around because it is so hard to find customers; no one wants to "fire them." Yet, when customers cost you more to serve than to keep, that is exactly what needs to be done.

Understanding the factors that lead to success in business is essential. Understanding the obstacles is equally important. The tools that enable management to do this are metrics—as well as the actions that must follow when metrics expose an area for management attention. The good news: Many of the necessary tools already exist, they just need to be adapted for a new purpose.

The Approach: Find It, Fix It, Use It or Lose It— and Keep It Simple

Global competition is tough. Markets are in a constant state of change, something that keeps customers nervous or at least uneasy. Take this occasion to go on a company "diet" of sorts. Prune low-profit, low-volume, and unnecessary products. Lose unprofitable customers. Assign those too small to be served economically to distributors—that is what distributors are for. Simplify your IT systems, too. Eliminate the outdated reports, unused screen formats, and obsolete software.

Just because you can make and/or sell a product or provide a service doesn't mean you should. How does it fit your strategic business plans? How does it help you achieve your goals and objectives? Treat complexity now—not later, or a more effective competitor will gain an advantage over you because of it.

First, you will need to recognize what constitutes complexity and the hidden costs it creates, and where it siphons off profit into blind alleys and hidden corners of the business. Next, you'll need to find it in your business and decide whether it creates or destroys value. Then, decide to either "Use It"—change structure and processes to capitalize on value-added complexity for competitive advantage—or "Lose It"—reduce or eliminate complexity that does not add value wherever it has crept into your business.

Finally, you will need to institute new metrics and modifications to existing management cost-control systems to know when to drive complexity out, and when to capitalize on it. Last, and most important: Keep the management of complexity as *simple* as possible, so whether you "use it or lose it" you solve the problem and keep it solved.

Why Have We Missed It?

It sounds so simple to recognize and fix complexity, doesn't it? Then why haven't more people in more companies in the past decade or two recognized the problem of complexity and fixed it? It's been there all along. People either don't see it, don't measure it, or don't believe how serious it is. And if and when they do, their corrective efforts are fleeting, and relapses are frequent.

When I began thinking about this problem, it seemed to me that there must be something, some factor getting in the way of stopping this runaway complexity. That same factor is burying people with work and frustration, while undermining companies' profits. What is that factor? The more I pondered what the factor is, the more it eluded me, until I realized that the problem was right before my eyes, but buried amidst . . . *more complexity.* Eureka! That was it. It was the Complexity Factor that complicates life and business, adding work while eroding profits.

No wonder we can't easily see complexity's impact. Every system we use to look at things obscures complexity, hides its effects, or puts its consequences in places where we either can't readily find them, or if we do, can't track them back to their root causes. When we do notice the adverse impact of complexity is at the end of the month, when we tally up all the revenue and expenses to see if we made money, and if so, how much. By then, there is nothing we can do to turn back the clock if we don't like what we see.

Accounting for Cause and Effect

Most companies account for every dollar that comes in and goes out in some kind of revenue or expense account. That isn't the problem. The problem is that few (or no) companies track why those dollars ended up in those accounts. Many of the accounts are catch-alls. Variances, those nasty little differences between what was supposed to happen (financially) and what actually happened, can contain hundreds of different types of entries. Each of these entries represents something gone awry.

Advocates of activity-based costing (ABC) might claim that it does track complexity costs, but it doesn't. While ABC may address costs more accurately than older, standard-cost accounting systems, only major changes in ABC will address the hidden costs of complexity, and even then it will miss some of them (since they don't fall into the "cost accounting" areas).

The second problem is that far too many companies are still hung up on closing the books and evaluating the results according to the old-fashioned calendar—at ends of months, quarters, and years. There is nothing wrong with doing that, too, but with today's information systems and real-time data-gathering capability, how about tallying things up each *day*? This is not only possible, but also practical, *if* it is built into the structure and processes. The more advanced companies know if they make money each and every day—or not. Then, instead of digging into problems four to six weeks after the fact, they can chase them down literally as they are happening and begin corrective action much, much sooner. The technology all exists. Use it! Track down and stop complexity-related waste faster; don't wait for some old-fashioned accounting calendar to show the effects and mandate action.

If the sheer volume of variances, special charges, etc. and the amount of dollars contained in such accounts isn't enough, consider the costs of just managing runaway complexity. Every product or service requires some kind of documentation to create it: a part number, a process routing, a bill of materials, a work instruction, a specification, or just a description. The more new products/services created, the more time, people, offices, computers, phones, supplies, supervision, and on and on, that it takes to create and maintain them. If the information isn't current and up-to-date, bad consequences can result.

Next, consider the impact of using multiple facility locations, or doing business in multiple countries using multiple legal entities. All result in another layer of complexity-related overhead and expenses. Even when accountants track the expenses that result from growing complexity, there is seldom a clear cause-and-effect analysis. That is a growing symptom of the Complexity Crisis.

In the next several chapters, we'll back up to consider how the Complexity Crisis has evolved, largely unnoticed or at least unmeasured. Also, as I explain the Complexity Crisis, I will introduce a series of small, but memorable, truths. I'll use the term "Truths about Complexity" to describe them and denote them with the acronym TAC. I hope these little TACs will stick in your mind.

PART ONE

The Problem

1

WHAT IS THE COMPLEXITY CRISIS?

The Dangers of Chasing High Growth in Low/No-Growth Markets

"Fools ignore complexity. Pragmatists suffer it. Some can avoid it. Geniuses remove it."
—Alan Perlis, computer scientist and Yale University professor

Most of the world's wealth is concentrated in developed markets like the United States, Europe, and Japan. However, most of the world's people are concentrated in the less-developed markets like China, India, Indonesia, Africa, etc. The people in these less-developed markets are poor. The most lucrative markets, where wealth is concentrated, are barely growing at all from a population perspective. Many have negative population growth, with too few births to offset the deaths. Japan, the United States. and most of Western Europe have aging populations and are facing huge social problems dealing with the costs of this demographic certainty.

When population isn't growing, markets are usually not growing either—or at least not very fast. When there is overcapacity for everything globally, prices come under pressure (i.e., they decline, or there is significant market pressure to lower them); thus, unit sales growth does not translate into financial growth. In spite of this, investment markets and owners of companies seek financial growth. They see lack of growth as a lack of vitality in a company. So, the pressure for growth builds. Companies routinely seek double-digit growth (in sales revenue) in markets that they admit are growing slowly or not at all. How do they expect to do this?

In a word: proliferation. They create more new products; sell them in more places; offer them in more varieties; source them from more, different, distant low-cost sources; and offer more services. There is just one problem with this scenario. The increase in sales happens, but profits don't go up, they go down. More products, more customers, more distribution channels, more suppliers—more, more, more of everything results in costs that grow at a far greater rate than the revenue.

An even worse situation occurs when a company caught up in its own ego attempts to grow in markets that seem to share attributes with its core market but are actually different, thus requiring a different set of core competencies and capabilities.

During my career, I was president of two well-known companies where I saw this happen. Huffy Corporation was the largest bike company in the world in the 1980s and 1990s. Huffy dominated in selling bicycles to the mass market. After a defensive move to block a competitor's acquisition of the Raleigh brand license for the U.S. dealer market resulted in Huffy obtaining the license, it decided to sell to the bicycle-dealer market, a very different type of distribution. Huffy concluded (incorrectly) that it could easily expand in the bicycle-dealer market by selling entirely different kinds of bicycles to these new and different customers. True, the products were still bicycles, but they were quite different in price, specification, retail outlets, distribution system, and especially in the buyers' purchase motivation and decision criteria. It turned out that while Huffy had core competencies in bicycles, it lacked the core capabilities—a deep understanding of the customer and consumer differences—needed to sell and service a dealer market, which was very different from a mass-retail market.

I watched this unfold from my spot as president of Huffy's (profit-able) "mass retail" bicycle division. We knew that our products were quite different from those carried by bike dealers. Consumers shopping at bike dealers wanted higher-spec products than sold in discount stores. The complexity from this and other differences came in layers: a differ-ent, more fragmented distribution system (dealer-distributor vs. one-step retail); a much less price-sensitive elitist consumer base; different products focused on high spec, light weight, performance, and "snob appeal." Finally, most bicycle dealers made relatively little of their profit on the bikes; most of their profit came from service and accessories.

Complexities like this lurk below the surface of many apparently similar businesses. Companies, hungry for new top-line growth, make this kind of mistake when entering "next-door markets" all the time. They underestimate the market-segment differences and overestimate their ability to understand and address them profitably. That leads down a path to financial failure—a common outcome of unrecog-nized complexity.

Rubbermaid was named "America's Most Admired Company" by *Fortune* magazine in the 1990s. During that era, I was group presi-dent of the office-products group—a multinational, predominantly business-to-business unit of Rubbermaid. Rubbermaid had built its company mostly selling retail/consumer trade channels. Like the pre-vious Huffy example, many products were alike, or at least largely so. They looked similar and performed the same basic functions (waste-baskets, for example), but the customers' purchasing choices were based on quite different criteria. Large industrial/commercial buyers had different needs than consumer markets. These seemingly subtle differences added unseen complexity—layers of structural, process, cultural, and relationship differences that were hard to even imagine until you encountered them.

The finer details were the factors that drove purchases, and these were different. Business buyers were concerned about easy and rapid supply, interchangeability within an office environment, compatibility with office décor, and, of course, price. Consumers either wanted pure function at the lowest price or fashionable decorative items for their home, kitchen, bath, etc. These seemingly similar needs were widely different and drove an explosion of complexity in products, colors, styles, distribution channels, and more.

Complexity Is Widespread—And Growing

In 2003, I spoke to a group of executives at Georgia Tech University. My topic was "The Curse of Complexity," a subject I had been interested in for some time. Several years earlier I had studied the field of scientific complexity and its application to business. During that time, I met with world-class biological scientist Stuart Kauffman at the Santa Fe Institute to discuss the topic of complexity. I have always recalled something that Stuart Kauffman told me as we sat in his mountaintop Santa Fe home and talked about the impact of complexity on our respective fields. "The adjacent possibilities [in the biological universe] are increasing at a tremendous rate," Kauffman said. My instinctive answer was, "The same is happening in the business world." His next sentence stuck in my mind: "It is beginning to exceed our ability to deal with them."

Since this conversation, the only difference is that the word "beginning" is no longer appropriate. Consider the sheer number of consumer choices. Observe the development of new enterprises in emerging countries. Look at the explosion of infotainment media and its dazzling convergence. The array of adjacent possibilities has dramatically increased, and when combined with the effects of technology and globalization, it is already exceeding the ability of management to deal with them.

The New Understanding

Was Kauffman right? I reflected on my three-plus decades as a working executive, consultant, and board member, and I concluded that he absolutely was, and the explosion of complexity is the evidence. Every company I worked with had exhibited problems of complexity—in products, in markets, in multiple locations, or in corporate entities (in different countries). I vividly recalled encountering these problems when I was a working executive, but had not connected them to complexity, per se. It became evident to me that new rules and new metrics were needed to deal with the increasing challenge of complexity because the old ones didn't work anymore—at least not sufficiently. Thus, my 2003 keynote speech at Georgia Tech—and the concept of this book—was born.

During a board meeting the year before, a fellow board member, Jack Shewmaker (formerly president and vice chairman of Wal-Mart), pointed out that the company had been growing nicely in sales but not in bottom-line profits. He related that he had seen this happen before, at Wal-Mart, during a period when management let the number of products, or SKUs (stock-keeping units), grow uncontrollably.

A large retail store, like a Wal-Mart Super Center, offers a huge variety of products—100,000 or more. The temptation is great to add products in hope of increasing sales, gaining an advantage on competitors, or simply trying fresh, new items. More SKUs took more effort—and cost—to manage, but that cost didn't show anywhere until the accounting period was over. Then it showed in terms of lower profits.

As the board discussed this, I realized that what he was talking about was runaway complexity, draining the efforts and diluting the focus of management, and eroding the profits of the company along with it. The goal of top-line sales-revenue growth was being pursued with runaway proliferation of products, customers, suppliers, and market segments served. No one was closing out the older, unproductive products with all of their related components. Worse yet, none of the accounting systems—standard costing, activity-based costing, or product/customer-profitability analyses—captured these costs of complexity, exposing them as a huge problem.

The adverse impact on profits manifested itself in higher variances (inventory excess/obsolescence, closeout pricing, repack/rework, premium freight charges, etc.) or overhead, SG & A (selling, general, and administrative expenses) and operations management (documentation, staffing, administration, etc.). Furthermore, the time delay in moving new items through the system increased as staff was too bogged down by an overload of SKUs, customers, markets, locations, etc., to create records, which then had to be maintained.

This reduction in speed of response creates a competitive disadvantage that is another unrecognized consequence of complexity. Not only does it slow down the responsiveness to customers, but it also slows down the selling and marketing efforts by forcing the company to concentrate on a larger number of offerings. Thus, complexity is also the enemy of speed, a critical success factor in today's fast-moving global competition.

HOW HIGH FASHION LED TO HIGH COMPLEXITY

Jack Shewmaker, a leading retail executive (now retired), once told me about a visit he made to a plant in Africa. This plant produced basic sportswear—particularly shirts and shorts—all of which were made of plain fabrics. The company had told Jack that for some reason, the plant was struggling and suffering financially. During his plant tour, Jack noticed one part of the plant where fabric inventory was piled high. He also noticed that over the course of the day, the "production lines" (such as they were) were constantly being interrupted—jobs were being set aside and different jobs started. This clearly hindered productivity.

When he inquired, first about the huge piles of fabric inventory, and then about the constant production interruptions, he was told, "It's for the new ladies' fashion-wear products. We must keep the many different fabrics because variety is important. Since we don't get much lead-time and the fabric suppliers want to produce quantity to keep the price down, we have to carry a lot of inventory. With our shirts and shorts, the demand is steady, the fabrics are simpler, fewer colors and styles are needed, and we buy more of it, so we just kept it flowing and don't have to stack it up 'just in case' we got an order. The quantities ordered of the fashion wear are smaller and we need to interrupt the production of our standard garments to run the dresses, etc. That is why there are so many production interruptions." Jack asked if that didn't make the dresses and fashion wear too costly to produce. The answer was, "Not really, because we spread the overhead evenly across all products." At that point, it was obvious to him why this plant was struggling both operationally and financially. The standard, high volume of basic goods was essentially subsidizing the more complex fashion lines, in terms of production costs and inventory needs.

Jack suggested that the company reconsider its decision to make the fashion wear, because its perceived higher prices and profit margins were not real. If they would assign costs to the correct places, including inventory costs and obsolescence, they would see that.

When he returned to visit this plant almost a year later, it had eliminated all but a few of the best-selling fashion items. The fashion items it kept were similar in construction to its other clothing, requiring just fabric, trim, and/or button changes. The company had its costs well under control and was operating profitably again.

Don't Preserve the Past—Find the Future

We are all a product of our past. We are also creatures of our present. Everything we have and do happens in the here and now. We know the future lies in front of us, but our reaction to it varies from enthusiasm to fear, from cynicism to compliance. Only the exceptional few actually think about how they can shape their own future. Since companies are social organizations populated and operated by human beings, they take on many characteristics of humanity. One such characteristic contributes to, and perhaps worsens, complexity more than many others. I describe it with a simple formula—the first TAC, or Truth about Complexity, that you'll encounter in this book.

TAC #1: A FORMULA FOR THE FUTURE

Here's a formula to consider:

$$PP \times 2 \neq FF$$

To put it another way: PP times 2 is *not* equal to FF.

What it means: Protecting/Preserving the Past (PP) and Perfecting the Present (PP) does not equal Finding the Future (FF).

Although everything you know is part of the past, and everything you live through now is part of the present, everything you will encounter for the rest of your life is part of the future—which is unpredictable, intimidating, or frightening. Thus, who could blame you for hanging onto your old—or current—favorites, be it products, services, customers, etc.? Also, if you don't work on perfecting the present, won't the (current) competition beat you?

Any business should look at the current landscape; however, if you spend all of your time, energy, thought, and resources on the past and the present, you and your organization will be left with no time or resources to Focus on, to Find, or to Fund the Future (all three are FFs). By which I mean, you won't have the resources—people, time, or money—to focus on new developments or emerging markets, find new customers or strategic partners, or fund innovation.

Companies cling to old products, often championed by their old customers, as they slide down the slope of the product life cycle into oblivion. You obsess about the present, investing more time and money on incremental improvements to current practices, products, programs, and services; and when you are done, you are drowning in complexity that is aging fast, and you have few (or no) resources left to Find, Fund, and Focus on the Future.

So, you proliferate. You try to sell lots of new and different stuff to new and different customers in new and different markets and maybe, if you are lucky, the top line—sales revenue—goes up. But the bottom line almost never does. It goes down and then, soon after, so does the top line—when the past winners finally die off and today's winners begin to falter.

In this book, I will describe how to recognize, contain, control, count, and manage complexity. Throughout the book, but especially in Part 2, "The Examples," I will describe how others have capitalized on complexity for competitive advantage or how some companies have chosen to eliminate complexity to make room for the new, the exciting, the future successes. I hope you will remember PP × 2 ≠ FF and what it means. The future is uncertain, but there is one certainty about it: *The rest of your life and your career from this day forth will be lived in the future.* It would be wise to make the most of it.

WHY IS IT A CRISIS NOW?

An Old Problem in New Clothing

"Complexity is not to be admired. It's to be avoided."
—Jack Trout, author and consultant

Proliferation is not a recent development. It is an old problem in new clothing—but one now driven by the explosion in information technology, globalization, and the search for high growth in low-growth markets. Complexity begets complexity. The Complexity Crisis is now so obvious to me that I continue to be amazed that it has remained widely unrecognized for so long. Over the past few years, my thoughts have evolved as I have seen a few companies react and do the right things to deal with complexity, but many, many more continue to struggle. Once I had considered the true nature of today's problem, I went back to Peter Drucker's work to test my hypothesis. Drucker wrote about concepts related to the Complexity Crisis in his classic 1963 *Harvard Business Review* article, "Managing for Business Effectiveness." In the summary, Drucker stated his beliefs.

"The end products of the manager's work are decisions and actions, rather than knowledge and insight. The crucial decision is the allocation of efforts. And no matter how painful, one rule should be adhered to: in allocating resources, especially human resources of high potential, the needs of those areas which offer great promise must first be satisfied to the fullest extent possible. If this means that there are no truly productive resources left for a lot of things it would be nice but not vital to have or to do, then it is better—much better—to abandon these uses, and not to fritter away high-potential resources or attempt to get results with low-potential ones. This calls for painful decisions, and risky ones. But that, after all, is what managers are paid for."

In essence, Drucker said that clarity of focus is critical in allocating resources, which is the essential job of management. Complexity destroys focus, and thus, is the natural enemy of focused resource allocation and good management. Marketing guru Theodore Levitt also weighed in around this time, in another classic *Harvard Business Review* article on innovation. Here is the essence of what he said:

People confuse "creativity" and "innovation." Management often mistakenly thinks that it can have a few brainstorming sessions, generate hundreds of "cool ideas," and call that innovation. Wrong. Ideation is the easy part. The hard part is sorting out which ones have the most merit and commercializing them successfully. Thus, the misguided search for innovation also compounds complexity.

Drowning in the Wrong Work

As I struggled with these principles in the "real world" of business for four decades, I began to see that these insights just scratch the surface.

A company that tries to chase too many ideas will only encounter another form of the Complexity Crisis, and drown in work, but not in profits. Over 90 percent of new product ideas fail in the marketplace—and that is after the "unproductive ideas" (from uncontrolled creativity sessions) have been eliminated. Imagine how dismal the failure rate would be if all of the ideas labeled "creative" were pursued into some form of commercialization. Of course they couldn't be, because the workload would inundate the best of organizations.

The hard part of innovation is sorting out which ideas should make the cut, and then undertaking the job of successfully commercializing them. When done right, creativity leads to wonderful breakthroughs, and it focuses the work of management on the right jobs. When done incorrectly, misguided creativity leads to disabling complexity.

Two examples of creativity involving Apple Computer will show two things: first, how Apple fell victim to complexity, and then much later, how it learned to avoid complexity—leading to great success.

Palm Pilot Versus Apple's Newton

More than a decade ago, Apple Computer created the first broadly available PDA (personal digital assistant)—a complex and powerful device called "the Newton." It did anything and everything. This complexity proved to be its blessing—and its curse.

The more functionality built into a product, the more the user must learn to take advantage of its capabilities. In the case of Newton, complexity also made the device large, power hungry, and expensive. Early adopters and dedicated techies loved it, but the general population of business users was unwilling to learn how to use all of its many features. The Newton survived for a short time and then faded into history.

Shortly thereafter, Palm introduced its first Palm Pilot. This device was one-third the size and weight of the Newton, significantly less costly, and at its core were two key functions: an electronic appointment calendar and a phone/contact directory. Other functions were simple and minimal—a to-do list, a calculator, and an alarm clock—all of which were intuitively simple to use. When Palm lost the complexity of the Newton, it found a huge market for a simpler, friendlier device. The Palm became the gold standard of PDAs, and millions were sold. It was created with software and a cradle to help synchronize its files with a computer—where a user could use the computer's power to "do the heavy lifting," letting the Palm do the simple tasks it did best. Simplifying the PDA—losing the complexity—made it a big success.

Apple and the iPod

A somewhat similar story evolved more recently, and once again, Apple was a participant. However, in the case of the iPod, Apple learned its lesson and got it right. While MP3 players of varying complexity already existed in an assortment of shapes and sizes, music downloads were an underground, borderline-illegal practice.

Perhaps Steve Jobs and the Apple innovation team learned from Sony's success with the Walkman a generation earlier, or perhaps they recalled the mistakes of the Newton. Whatever the genesis, Apple created a simple, single-function music player—the iPod. The design was elegant and the controls were user friendly, because there was not a lot of complexity to control. Choose the album and song, set the volume, and play, pause, rewind, or fast-forward. This latter set of commands was so familiar from the Walkman era that little learning was required. But then there were literally dozens, maybe hundreds of competing MP3 players out there. Why did the iPod win so dramatically?

The short answer is a combination of elegant design and simplicity. Apple did this by focusing on what consumers wanted and valued. Complexity was avoided by not trying to make the iPod all things to all people. As millions of people have purchased iPods, the users have recognized other data can be stored in its memory—photos, videos, addresses, and more—but Apple didn't push that complexity at first. Apple focused on music and avoided complexity.

The user did have to download music via their computer onto the iPod, but here Apple's simple plug and play Macintosh computers and iTunes software made that easy too (another potential complexity avoided). Rip a CD using your Mac's iTunes software, then drag and drop it onto a playlist and/or the iPod icon. Voilà—you have music both on your iPod and on your computer.

But Steve Jobs and company saw a much broader, different, yet still simple vision. Don't try to deal with the complexity and prospective illegality of pirated music. Napster was under attack for the illegal copying of music and helping users share songs at no cost. Other similar Web sites and systems were similarly labeled "pirates." The objective was simple: Fill the need for an easy place to get music—without becoming part of an Internet piracy scheme. Apple realized that a great opportunity existed if it could forge an agreement to sell individual songs and entire albums, rewarding artists and music companies with part of the sale proceeds. A deal was made and the iTunes Music Store was born, joined at the hip with the iPod and Mac iTunes software. This was another victory over complexity, and one that put Apple and the iPod over the top.

What was born with the iPod and iTunes became a huge and growing success story. What was this success based on? Focused simplicity's victory over complexity created this success. Apple adroitly kept the number of models of iPod to a few.

Then Apple took another step of eliminating complexity while lowering cost of entry with the introduction of the $99 iPod Shuffle. This iPod was even simpler, since it used flash memory—etched on a chip instead of a mini hard drive with the many tiny, mechanical moving parts. Although it also lost some of the larger, more expensive iPod control features, the Shuffle replaced them with just two simple choices—play the songs in the order they are stored or shuffle them randomly (hence the name). Eliminating complexity from an already simple design was a success again as the iPod Shuffle's $99 price point opened a much larger market for potential sales—especially among youthful music fans. Sales zoomed.

Apple reduced complexity again the next year by discontinuing the iPod Mini, despite its popularity, and introduced the improved, smaller, and more technologically simple (and "cooler") iPod, the Nano. Somehow, once a company understands losing complexity, that company can replicate its success even when others struggle to do the same thing. The enticing tendency to add more features adds complexity, inflates cost, and can create user resistance.

Apple's elegantly simple iPod model assortment opened the iPod world to millions of music enthusiasts, to technophobes, and to pre-teens. No matter the budget, iPods fed people's widely varying taste for more music. Where do they get the music? They buy it from Apple's iTunes Music Store at 99 cents a song. Simple? You bet. Successful? You know it.

What Apple accomplished with the iPod provides a lesson worth learning. New products are wonderful, but all have defined life cycles: growth, maturity, and then decline. Only the most courageous and foresighted companies dare to "kill" (phase out and replace) a successful product *before* it has peaked and headed into decline. The very best innovators, like Steve Jobs and Apple, replace a good product with a new one, using an even better technology. By doing this, Apple averted complexity's greatest threats. The number of product variations was controlled without limiting the product's volume potential or the market excitement around it. Auto companies could learn a lot from Apple's iPod strategy.

THE BOTTOM LINE—
WHERE COMPLEXITY HURTS

An Example that Will Hit Close to Home

> *"A man who carries a cat by the tail learns something he can learn in no other way."*
> —Mark Twain

The expression "the bottom line" has become common in our language to describe a final outcome in a short phrase. The origin of the bottom line as vernacular comes from the income statement—the accounting report used to show the profitability of a company—which shows the net income on its bottom, or last, line.

As companies struggle for growth in sales revenue, they try to drive the "top line," which is where sales revenue shows on the income statement. Thus the term "top-line growth" has become increasingly synonymous with a goal for companies that are appreciated by Wall Street stock markets for their revenue growth—which it assumes will be translated into increased profit (net income—the bottom line) growth.

Nearly all companies seem to be struggling for top-line growth these days. A lack of top-line growth (and the associated bottom-line growth) is perceived as a sign of weakness in a business and leads to investor concern. Many companies succeed in gaining that top-line growth, but do it the wrong way, introducing costly complexity along with the growth.

When the results are compiled at the end of a month or quarter, only then do they discover that the top line may have indeed gone up nicely, but the bottom line went down—often dramatically down. The common question, asked in a panic-stricken voice, is "How could this have happened?" Here is an explanation and an example of just how this happens. The outcome of such a real-life situation is, indeed, the Complexity Crisis in its most common form.

Background for Nonfinancial Readers

For those of you not familiar with financial statements, I'll explain the two most important ones briefly. Understanding these basic accounting statements will make it easier to see how costs due to complexity remain hidden until too late. For those of you who are accounting literate, please excuse my oversimplifications, which are done in the interest of clarity.

The Income Statement (P and L)

The income statement is often called "the P and L" (profit and loss). It is intended to summarize the revenue of a company or business unit, then subtract from it all of the costs and expenses and other accounting charges related to that revenue until what's left (it hopes) is some profit—"net income"—which is commonly shown as the bottom line.

The Balance Sheet

The balance sheet is an accounting statement where the assets and liabilities of the company are tallied and then forced to balance by the addition of a positive or negative number for shareholder equity. The most commonly looked at lines on a balance sheet are cash on hand; accounts receivable (what customers owe the company); inventory; accounts payable (what the company owes suppliers); property, plant, and equipment (facilities, equipment, and other tangible assets); and debt (which may take multiple lines to show as short-term, long-term, etc.). Finally, there is also a bottom line on the balance sheet. This is a positive or negative number representing shareholder equity (or some similar name), which is the accumulation of prior income (or losses) that makes it balance, thus the name balance sheet.

This is a grossly oversimplified description, but is intended to get all readers on a common level of understanding, even those who are not financial wizards. Most businesses have accounting periods during which transactions are accumulated; booked (entered); and, at the end of the month, quarter (three months), and year, tallied up to show how well the business did financially. These are usually reviewed by executives and managers responsible for compiling them, and then shared with the rest of the organization and shareholders.

You as Part of the Organization

Take whatever role you find yourself in—the head of a business, the manager of a function, a professional working in that function, an employee working at another level in the company, a prospective investor, or perhaps the CFO (chief financial officer) or CEO (chief executive officer) reviewing the most recent accounting period's P and L.

Income Statement: The Complexity Factor, Inc.

(All $ in thousands)	Q1-Actual	% Sales	Q1-Plan	%Sales	Variance	Change +/-
Gross Sales Revenue	163,550	107.63%	150,000	106.57%	13,550	9.0%
Claims & Deductions	9,037	5.95%	7,000	4.97%	2,037	29.1%
Other Customer Charges	1,251	0.82%	1,000	0.71%	251	25.1%
Terms Discounts	1,300	0.86%	1,250	0.89%	50	4.0%
Net Sales	**151,962**	**100.00%**	**140,750**	**100.00%**	**11,212**	**8.0%**
Standard Cost of Goods						
Material	65,780	43.29%	60,000	42.63%	5,780	9.6%
Labor	7,110	4.68%	6,500	4.62%	610	9.4%
Overhead	24,950	16.42%	22,000	15.63%	2,950	9.4%
Freight-out	11,416	7.51%	10,000	7.10%	1,416	13.4%
Shipping Expenses	3,750	2.47%	3,000	2.13%	750	14.2%
Total Cost of Goods Sold (COGS)	113,006	74.36%	101,500	72.11%	11,506	25.0%
Standard Gross Profit Margin	38,956	25.64%	39,250	27.89%	(294)	11.3%
Variances	2,925	1.92%	150	0.11%	2,775	-2.3%
Gross Profit Margin	**36,031**	23.71%	**39,100**	27.78%	**(3,069)**	4.1%
Selling Expenses	15,697	9.60%	13,900	9.27%	1,797	12.9%
G&A Expenses	12,379	7.57%	10,200	6.80%	2,179	21.4%
Total SG&A Expenses	28,076	17.17%	24,100	16.07%	3,976	16.5%
EBIT (Earnings Before Interest & Taxes)	**7,955**	5.23%	**15,000**	10.66%	**(7,045)**	**-47.0%**
Nonrecurring Expenses	1,200	0.79%	250	0.18%	950	380.0%
Interest Expense	5,490	3.61%	4,390	3.12%	1,100	25.1%
Other Income/Expense	980	0.64%	10	0.01%	970	9700.0%
Taxes	260	0.17%	1,350	0.96%	(1,090)	-80.7%
Net Income	**25**	0.02%	**9,000**	6.39%	**(8,975)**	**-99.7%**

Sales Are Up!

Imagine you are sitting in a conference room, the graphics projector is on and the handouts are in everyone's hands, along with morning coffee. The presentation starts. The top-line revenue on the P and L shows gross sales revenue up 9 percent over plan (which was not much different from last year's number). It's not quite up to the desired 10 percent growth, but close. The hard-fought 4 to 5 percent price increase (largely charged to the older, loyal customers) went through, and that accounts for almost half of the increase. The rest is expected from the many new products and new customers the company has added in the past few months as part of its growth initiative.

Deductions Are Up, Too

The next two lines, "claims and deductions" and "other customer charges," are up too, and that's not so good. It seems that some of the new customers are taking unwarranted deductions and some of the older ones are making claims because of errors made by sales or distribution. Some are misunderstandings on the new "hot deals" used to get the price increase accepted—and others are caused by errors of the overworked people trying to get all the last-minute orders (especially the new ones) out at the end of the quarter. The quarter end is important because that's when Wall Street has projected earnings to be up, like sales, about 10 percent.

In our example, the 9 percent gross-sales gain has already been reduced to 8 percent by higher-than-expected claims, deductions, and other charges for problems—mostly complexity driven—and that's not good, since the top-line growth was already short of Wall Street's 10 percent expectations.

COGS Is Up, Margins Are Down

The next group of lines represents the COGS (cost of goods sold). When subtracted from net sales, it leads to the gross profit margin. These lines include costs of the material, labor, overhead, and freight/shipping associated with the products produced/procured this quarter, most of which were either sold in the quarter or will sell in the next quarter (or will remain in inventory until sold). When the total of these lines is subtracted from net sales, what's left is the gross profit margin—the profit made on the sales based on the standard costs set at the start of the budget (fiscal) year.

Here, too, there is a mishap. It seems that the assortment—the mix of products sold—was not nearly the same as planned. The push for growth caused the actual mix of products and customers to shift to the new, lower-margin products and customers, and that further eroded the profit margin. Not only that, but it looks like the overhead expenses (due to that mix shift) were higher than normal too, reducing gross margin still more. The final gross margin as a percentage of sales is now noticeably below budget. In the quiet, someone in the room whispers, "Look, margins are way down!"

Variances Are Up

Next, right below the "Standard Gross Profit Margin" line, there is a single line titled "Variances," and the explanation by the controller is that they, too, are unfavorable (which means negative). Variances are expenses that result when actual expenses are different from what was in standards, or when there are unusual charges/events that were not planned at all. When combined with the increased claims and deductions, almost one-quarter of the profit from the 8 percent revenue growth has disappeared. Hmmm. This is not so good and promises to get worse. The explanation is that the variances were mostly due to rework and scrap associated with the new products, but some of it was also from reimbursing vendors for expedited freight—airfreight from China—to get replacement goods for the rejects the new vendors shipped. Once again, for a moment, the room is deadly quiet, until another whisper breaks the silence, "Wow, look at that variance line!"

It seems that the company's hastily developed new product specs weren't clear enough for the new Asian vendor (the old supplier knew about these quirks, but wasn't willing to bid a low-enough price), and while the products shipped can be reworked and repacked, that will take too much time. Thus, the company must foot the bill for premium freight cost because the specs were incomplete and not clear. These are big bucks and costly mistakes. Is any of this sounding familiar yet?

SG&A Is Up, Too

Selling expenses are up as a percentage of sales, because the reps were given an incentive—higher commissions—to sell new products to new accounts. The sales rep costs went up, even though the products they sold were cheaper than the old ones. Marketing expenses are up too because of advertising costs required to launch products in new trade channels, but that was part of the deal promised to new customers to get them to switch suppliers—to your company. Next comes the G&A section of SG&A (selling, general, and administrative). Here's more bad news. Fixed G&A costs are up, since those include insurance costs, which have been climbing because of the new business operations set up to serve new distribution in Florida (hurricane country), on the West Coast, and in Canada (new international regulations). Then there are the costs of establishing a new legal entity in Canada, and some start-up fees for customs-related matters on the new imported products. Of course, utility costs are up, especially energy-related costs, because the company uses natural gas, and the rapid growth didn't allow time to negotiate new, cost-effective gas-supply agreements. There go a couple more percentage points of our top-line revenue increase. Ouch.

EBIT Is Down—Way Down

This gets us to the EBIT line. EBIT stands for "earnings before interest and taxes," and it is intended to portray the normal-time-period earnings before the impact of interest, taxes, and nonrecurring expenses. It is now way short of budget targets. Half of the profit gain from the 8-percent top-line revenue growth has disappeared, and we aren't to the bottom line yet, either.

Interest and Other Expenses Are Up, Too

Below the EBIT line are three large entries. The largest one is "interest expense," which is way up, because inventories are higher (to feed the wider variety of new products to the less familiar array of new customers). Forecast errors have been big, and each time, more and different inventory has to be ordered from Asian suppliers with a lead-time of sixty to ninety days. Remember, to fill the first round of customers' orders on a timely basis, airfreight was needed. The amount of airfreight premium could have been lowered by short-shipping our older, loyal customers (and then apologizing profusely while they waited, hoping they'd just tolerate the shortages and delays)—but that's a bad idea too.

Other Income/Expenses Are Up, Too—the Expenses Part

The next largest entry is "Nonrecurring Expenses," and it is another biggie. What for? To open the new facilities, hire and relocate the new sales reps, and set up businesses in new countries and even states like Florida and California. There's one small problem. This group may be called "nonrecurring" but if you expand this way again, there'll be another set of these charges, and another after that, so they will "recur." Oh yes, you forgot to budget for a couple of new taxes levied on the inventory stored in California too. Just a little "icing on the cake."

The final "Other Income/Expense" line also shows a big expense over budget! The bad news just doesn't stop. It seems intellectual property pirates registered the company's brand name and Web domain name in a couple of those new foreign markets and you had to buy them back. Nobody thought about budgeting for something like this as part of the international expansion. Finally, there is the "Taxes" line, which includes the unexpected taxes on inventory, but no taxes on income—because there isn't any left!

The Top Line Was Up, but the Bottom Line Is Gone!

Here we are: the bottom line. Net income on over $13 million of gross sales and $11+ million more of net sales is . . . $25,000? Right, it is $25,000.

"*What?*" The roomful of stunned people gasps in surprise. "That can't be right," mumbles one midlevel manager. "We were supposed to make $9 million more!"

"Oh, it's right," says the controller. "And worse yet, we are now two weeks into the second quarter and it appears to be continuing on the same track as the first quarter."

"But everyone is working like crazy to get the new products, new customers, and new locations going," adds another disbelieving participant.

"I know," answers the controller. "It seems that all the sales growth and any profits expected from it have been eaten up by the complexity we added. Worst of all, the costs and margins looked good at first. All of these hits came in accounts where the causes were hidden until we dug into them."

As the group files out of the conference room in a stunned silence, the seasoned assistant to the young CFO rests her hand on his arm and quietly says, "My, what a shame . . . and after everyone worked so hard, too."

What a Shame, Indeed

All the expected increase in profit from the sizable growth in sales revenue is gone, eaten up by unplanned, unexpected, and largely hidden costs—until the month-end and quarter-end statements were compiled. The product pricing and margin looked a little narrow, but not that bad. It was just that nobody considered the economic impact of complexity of new customers, new products, new distribution, new suppliers, working from new specs, doing business in new states and countries with different regulations and legal practices, and added costs of relocation, special commissions, freight, and so forth. And all of this was made worse by trying to do it all "too fast." The Complexity Crisis occurs in many ways, and all of them seem to be both painful and hidden from management control systems until too late.

The Balance Sheet Suffers, Too

If we were to review the balance sheet of this company, we'd see inventories above plan because all the new products are finally arriving from offshore—the right ones *and* the wrong ones. The reserve for obsolescence also will be higher, reducing the value of the inventory, because some of the forecasts were wrong, but the goods initially forecast will be arriving any day, too. Next accounting period will need to include forecasts of lower margins to close out these items.

Accounts receivable are also higher. It seems the customers have held back part of their payments until the claims and deductions can be resolved. The older, more loyal customers are balking too. You shipped late and incomplete, so they'll just pay a little late. It's interesting how complexity can hit all parts of the company, one way or another.

What Happened? Answer: The Complexity Crisis!

The Complexity Crisis struck this company as it has so many others—and it didn't even see the hit coming. In boxing, fighters say that the punch they don't see coming is the one that knocks them out. Perhaps business and boxing aren't that much different in this respect.

The scenario I have just outlined was not a real company, but it was a composite of real incidents I've seen as an executive, a consultant, and a board member. And all of those things really do happen, and far too often, they happen at the same time. A later chapter will describe how widely used accounting systems track direct product costs, but miss—and in fact hide—the costs that are incurred due to complexity. Before we go there, let's consider some of the other unintended consequences of complexity—the ones that impact a business in different ways.

UNINTENDED CONSEQUENCES

Complexity—the Enemy of Quality, Service, and Branding

"Most of what we call 'management' consists of making it difficult for people to get their work done."
—Peter F. Drucker

Practitioners of "statistical quality assurance" understand that the goal of consistently good quality is dependent on the reduction of variability. In naturally occurring events, and especially in the processing of materials by machinery, natural variation in dimensions and characteristics will occur. These are measurable, and if the variation of a dimension or characteristic is plotted and no adjustments are made to the process or machinery, this variation will take the shape of a bell curve—called a "normal statistical distribution."

The Bell Curve of Standard Statistical Distribution

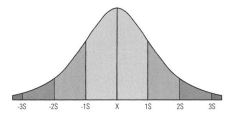

-3S   -2S   -1S   X   1S   2S   3S

Many metrics and parameters can be used to describe this normal distribution, the most famous of which is the standard deviation, described by the Greek letter *sigma*. The lowercase *sigma* (σ) is the common symbol for standard deviation, which is used to designate the variation in the normal distribution of measurements for a given process. The widely used term "six sigma" refers to a slice of the bell-shaped curve that encompasses six standard deviations—a variability that results in only 3.4 nonconformances out of 1 million measured characteristics. (The 1S, 2S, 3S shown on the figure stand for "1 sigma, 2 sigma, etc." although the correct designation is the Greek letter *sigma,* σ)

A six-sigma distribution does not equal perfection, but it's not far from it, and it is very hard to achieve. Complexity that is introduced into any process (and all businesses are essentially processes) creates variability, which is the natural enemy of consistent quality. But how and why does complexity create this variability that works against quality? Here's how.

Multiple Suppliers Cause More Variability

If there is one supplier of a given item, using one process, natural variation will occur as a result of that particular machine, method, etc. This variation, if measured in the output of the process or machine, and plotted as a graph, will result in a standard distribution or bell curve. Since most specifications call for a given performance metric, dimension, characteristic, etc., the middle of that bell curve (the median) or the average of the values plotted in the bell curve (the mean) is the target value, and there is normally a tolerance range + or - around that nominal target. As long as the items produced fall within that acceptable tolerance range of the target, they are in conformance—and usable.

But when the process varies more (a wider bell curve), some items produced fall outside the acceptable tolerance range and are considered nonconforming (or defective). These nonconforming items are usually not acceptable and must be sorted out, otherwise they might not work properly in subsequent steps down the line. Thus, the quest of quality is the reduction of variability in processes, such that as few as possible nonconforming items are created.

One process is easier to improve than several. One process is easier to keep in control than several, too. However, when a company uses multiple processes and/or multiple suppliers—even with each of them aiming at the *same* targets for dimensions—an unsettling thing happens. Each process and supplier might actually produce items that fall within the target range of acceptable variation.

For a simple example of how this works, imagine carryout coffee cups and lids. When one supplier makes both the lids and the cups, the fit can be quite precise—just tight enough to stay on, but not too difficult to put the lid on the cup. If there are two or three suppliers of both cups and lids, and only minor variations in size occur, all are within specifications; but when the largest lid is placed on the smallest cup, it comes off too easily, risking spills. When the smallest lid is placed on the largest cup, it is so tight that it's difficult to put on without damaging either the lid or the cup. All of the suppliers were within the specified size ranges, but the variability of the multiple suppliers' processes made the combinations undesirable—perhaps unacceptable.

Even when all of the products are within the acceptable range of tolerances, the shapes of each of the bell curves are different—simply because processes vary. The width of the bell curves may also be different. Unless the user segregates the items by supplier (which defeats the purpose of having interchangeable sources), the product combination must now accommodate the variation of multiple bell curves.

Multiply this effect by many parts from many sources (not just lids and cups), and then use those parts in different processes, each of which introduces new variability, and complexity's role in creating crises, by undermining quality, becomes painfully evident.

Titleist—Doing It Right Every Time

Titleist makes, arguably, the best golf balls—at least more competitive golfers must think so, since Titleist balls are by far the most popular golf balls in both professional and amateur tournaments. A Titleist ball (one version at least) consists of a core and a cover. (There are also multilayer balls, but the same principles apply.) The core is made of an elastomer—think of a synthetic rubberlike compound—which is mixed in large batches. The cover is a thin molded plastic shell that is fused around the core.

Let's consider the core only. Performance consistency is one of the characteristics desirable in a golf ball. That means that each ball behaves exactly the same way when struck by a club. The hardness and ability of the elastomer core to rebound plays a large role in this consistency. That means each core must be exactly the same hardness and must rebound from being hit (compressed) in exactly the same way. But there are multiple batches of core compound being produced.

Even a minute variation in the chemicals in the batches, or fluctuations in the temperature and the mixing process, might result in a core compound that has different characteristics from one batch to the next. When this material is molded under heat and pressure into a spherical shape, the temperature, pressure, time, and dimensions of the mold can vary. And there are multiple molds with multiple cavities, and each cavity is minutely different, and those small variations in pressure and temperature are often dependent on nothing more than the age and condition of the mold and the machine holding it. All of these variables determine the performance of the core, which in turn determines the performance of the ball. That's why making the best golf balls is very difficult.

Does the impact of variability start to make sense now? Titleist carefully monitors the consistency and performance characteristics of each batch of elastomer to assure that it will compress and rebound in exactly the same way. It does that by using bell-curve statistical analysis to understand not only whether the material is at the targeted characteristic, but also how much it might vary from batch to batch. The molds and machines, the temperatures, pressures, and time of the molding cycles must be (and are) very carefully controlled, monitored, recorded, and plotted. Knowing how the components and the processes vary allows the best control of the final product's conformance to Titleist's strict standards.

Now imagine that many different kinds of golf balls are made each day. Some are different models, with different performance characteristics, with cores in a variety of sizes and hardnesses, multilayer cores, different cover materials of varying thicknesses, hardnesses, and dimple patterns. You can see how dangerous a proliferation of too many ball types would be for Titleist. To its credit, Titleist has done it right. It has an appropriate range of balls, but constantly works to keep the range as narrow as possible and still fulfill the needs of golfers of all skill levels, as the world's leading golf-ball manufacturer must. When a company builds its competitive position on quality and consistency, complexity can be a deadly disease.

Service Is Impacted by Complexity, Too

Forecasts will be wrong. Why? Forecasts are predictions about the future, which is unknown. The more volatile the situation is—such as demand for a product that is weather dependent—the greater the likelihood of forecast error. The more items the forecast must predict, the more chances to make errors. The more locations where the demand originates, the more chances for error. The more people involved in the forecasting process, the more accurate it is—not. The more customers for whom demand must be forecast, the greater chance of error. This is why complexity adds to forecast error, and forecast error undermines customer service.

In fairness, there are often compensating or offsetting errors, but in today's environment, in which everyone wants his or her own unique version of everything, even that is less likely a benefit. Logistics experts and marketing planners search endlessly for the best forecasting systems, algorithms, and methods. There are some good ones out there, too. But those will also be wrong. Why? Because they are guesses, however educated, about an uncertain future. That means that in order to service a volatile demand from a customer there are only three solutions upon which to draw:

1. Carry more inventory—but it will inevitably contain the wrong stuff.
2. Get more lead-time—but that is usually neither acceptable nor possible.
3. Have more, flexible production capacity—in order to respond to forecast errors and changes in demand as rapidly as possible.

Some combination of the three is often used to yield the best service level. Number three is the best option, since numbers one and two are either impractical or error prone.

Now think about this: complexity leads to more of everything—products, customers, suppliers, markets, service, and so on. Inevitably, then, forecast errors will be magnified, and as a result, service will decline even though inventory probably goes up. That is how service becomes a victim of the Complexity Crisis.

Another Unintended Consequence—Brands Can Be Damaged, Too

Quality, service, costs—all are damaged by complexity. What next? Brands, that's what. How are brands harmed by complexity? That's simple. A brand is a promise of a value package embodied in a product or service. A brand is also a relationship in which consistency is a major element. When there is rampant proliferation of products, services, and everything surrounding them, there is also confusion in the mind of the customer and/or consumer. This confusion undermines the brand's promise of the package of value by adding doubt. It also raises questions about the stability of the brand relationship and the expected consistency accompanying that relationship. Finally, since a brand stands for something, stretching that brand across too many products, countries, markets, etc. blurs and ultimately undermines the identity of that brand. Some of the world's best brands struggle with this challenge of complexity.

Is a Hampton Inn a Hilton? Is Embassy Suites a Hilton? Is the vaunted Waldorf-Astoria a Hilton? The answer to all three is "yes."

But how could you know that? In these cases, the hidden connection with Hilton does little good and may actually dilute the brand (with the exception of the prestigious Waldorf-Astoria, where I stayed several times before realizing it was a part of Hilton, and I needed to include my Hilton Honors number when checking in).

Does McDonald's stand for Big Macs, hamburgers, fries, and Egg McMuffins, or does it stand for sliced fruit, a variety of salads, and occasional deli-style sandwich, or what?

Do you see the kind of disconnect in the mind of the consumer that complexity causes when a brand is involved? The brand has an image and a character or identity associated with it—and like a pat of butter, the further you spread it, the thinner it gets. If it gets too thin, it doesn't stand for much of anything anymore. That's why, more than two decades ago, Jack Trout and Al Ries, who wrote *Positioning: The Battle for Your Mind*, tried to discourage overextending brands and products associated with them. When the complexity strikes, it can damage or kill a brand.

Globalization and other business environmental effects (e.g., the Internet) of the past decade have created a much greater likelihood of complexity causing such a "perfect storm" of problems, both economic and operational. Add to that the wonders of globalization, and who knows what can happen. I recall an old saying that used to make me grin: "To err is human. To really screw up requires a computer." I could now add, "To make it really hard to fix, put a big ocean and ten to twelve time zones in the way." That's the subject of the next chapter. In a later chapter, I'll cover the human-organizational complexities of how we organize and do the work, which also compounds the Complexity Crisis.

WHAT MAKES IT WORSE?

Globalization and Latent Overcapacity
Add More Complexity

"That which does not destroy us makes us stronger."
—Friedrich Nietzsche, German philosopher

Globalization is a wonderful and challenging development. We can send information, purchase specifications, and orders around the world in seconds. Shipments, however, are still limited by the laws of physics and take much longer. Services can move more quickly. Call centers, back-office work, medical transcription, customer service, and accounting can be set up halfway around the world in a matter of weeks or even, when necessary, days.

The rub is that the problems that arise from such arrangements also get sent halfway around the world—and the difficulty in solving them becomes exponentially greater from that distance. Outsourcing via "offshoring" can be a powerful competitive weapon, but like all weapons, it requires learning its proper use before the skill is developed.

This global flexibility and the latent available capacity for almost everything facilitate the front end of outsourcing. I call it latent because even if capacity to do (or make) "whatever" doesn't exist now, it can be put into place very quickly if a demand arises. Yet this capability also increases vulnerability to the Complexity Crisis. Problems don't go away when they are moved far away to a new home. They just become harder and more expensive to solve.

Sell Everyone, Everything, Everywhere

In my previous P and L scenario, one possibility is that the sales force was given the following marching orders: "Get out there and get the sales growth. It's a big world." "There are lots of potential customers out there," is how one of my former bosses put it when he was pressing for unrealistic growth targets. "Now go find them. Sell everyone, everywhere, everything." And so we tried, and sometimes we did. The results were horrible.

Someone else had to get (procure or produce) the new products to supply the new customers in new places, and do it in a big hurry. And they did, because they were threatened with career-limiting consequences. The results (surprise?) were also horrible. "Haste makes waste" is a simple but accurate way to state what happens in such a situation.

Longer, More Complex Supply Chains, and Less Time to Respond

Another problem of globalization and complexity is that forecasts will be wrong, and when they are, the faster change occurs and the wider the range of options involved, the greater the forecast errors will be. The TAC (Truth about Complexity) below was shown in short form in the previous chapter. It bears repeating here. Few efforts are less productive than searching for solutions that do not exist. Instead, focus efforts on the effective use of solutions that are known.

TAC #2: ONLY THREE SOLUTIONS FOR WRONG FORECASTS

1. **Carry inventory as a hedge**—but it will be at least partly the wrong inventory, and it costs money to carry it and more money to dispose of the wrong stuff.
2. **Get more lead-time from customers**—but sometimes customers cannot or will not provide more lead-time, or competitors will offer shorter lead-times.
3. **Have more, flexible production capacity available**—which is clearly the best option of the three if you can afford it, and if it isn't so far away that it takes too long to get the goods where you need them, when you need them.

That's it. Anything else is a combination or variation of these three.

The longer a supply chain extends, and the more complex it is in makeup, the slower it will react to changes. And since change is the only certainty, what the supply chain delivers will invariably be wrong, and the more pressure to change, the more mistakes are made. Then the fun begins—repack, rework, haggle, closeout—all of which show up somewhere in the accounting system (often in variances), but not in the direct cost of the product involved. The new products still look like they are earning handsome margins. At the end of the accounting period—the month, the quarter, or the fiscal year—there will be large unfavorable entries in variances and other costs (freight, for one example, to deliver the right products via premium freight).

Expect inventories, especially the obsolete and noncurrent portion, to also be out of line (up).

If everything works fine and the forecast needs turn out to be reasonably accurate (this happens now and then), perhaps complexity will not be as large a problem. But, dealing with new suppliers thousands of miles away, who live and work in totally different countries and cultures, with different languages and business practices, is still likely to cause major complexity-related problems. Be prepared to deal with them.

TWO ESSENTIAL STEPS

Define the Problem First, Solve It Second

"Opportunity is missed by most people because it is dressed in overalls and looks like work."
—Thomas A. Edison

There are two steps to solving any problem: 1) Define the problem; 2) Solve the problem. It's awfully easy for an aggressive manager to jump right to step two, skipping step one almost entirely. That's a mistake. As companies struggle to compete in this pressure-packed environment, proliferation of everything is pervasive. Proliferation with a purpose is dangerous. Unintended and unmanaged proliferation can be fatal.

TAC #3: TWO STEPS TO SOLVE ANY PROBLEM

1. Define the problem.

2. Solve the problem.

The problem in this case is relatively simple to state. Companies are adding complexity faster than they are improving their ability to recognize it, measure it, or manage it. An appropriate pre-problem-solving step might be to "understand the problem." Growth is difficult when markets aren't growing. As markets grow at low, single-digit rates and companies try to grow at double-digit rates, they proliferate everything—products, services, customers, markets, distribution channels, facilities, etc.—creating unmeasured and unchecked complexity. It is crippling them instead of helping them. But it can work for them, or at least be managed so that it doesn't work against them. Unfortunately, that is not the norm.

WHARTON SURVEY CONFIRMS COMPLEXITY PROBLEM

In an online survey of 424 executives from more than thirty industry groups by Knowledge@Wharton (reported by the George Group), roughly half of the respondents indicated that portfolio complexity has a "'negative or a somewhat negative impact' on cost competitiveness and lead-time at their companies." Also from the report of this study: "A key finding of the survey was that, for a majority of the respondents—64 percent—a small portion of products and/or services account for all the operating profit at their companies. But even among those who claim complexity boosted profits at their companies, a fairly large number—38 percent—said the drivers were still a small portion of their products or services."

This problem also presents a great opportunity. The opportunity is to understand what we are doing and devise ways to make complex things simpler or make that complexity create competitive advantage. Southwest Airlines made the complex airline business simpler by using one plane type, one seating arrangement, one meal program (none), and flying point to point. Dell Computer made the production of an infinite variety of complex personal computers work more effectively by using the Internet for ordering and configuration, bundling subassemblies and options for corporate customers, locating key suppliers nearby, linking them tightly with a customized assembly line built around common design platforms and JIT (just-in-time) delivery. This was not a revolutionary new idea, just a new adaptation of an old idea, using Internet ordering as the enhancement. IBM did almost the same thing in Lexington, Kentucky, decades earlier in its production plant for Selectric® typewriters (a company that later became Lexmark).

The popular cliché is that these are increasingly complex times. Experts like Stuart Kauffman confirm this in the scientific world beyond a doubt; therefore, we should not expect the business world to be that much different. Dealing with this complexity compounded by the digital revolution and rapidly expanding globalization is also a necessity for today's managers. In the Special Report cited earlier on the Wharton survey, about 85 percent of the respondents admitted that the number of offerings at their companies have grown by at least 10 percent over the past five years. Half reported a more than 50 percent growth in offerings. I'd bet many respondents guessed at the number and their guesses were way lower than an analysis would reveal. Why? Because most companies have entire departments devoted to creating new products, and few or none are devoted to rationalizing product assortments and eliminating old products.

Based on personal experience answering surveys, and since I have begun questioning companies about this topic, I have found that most companies don't keep these kinds of statistics on a current basis. Thus I suspect (with good reason) that half of the respondents estimated many of their answers and had no (accurate) quantitative information showing how much their offerings had actually grown. I'd also bet that the half of the respondents who admitted 50 percent or more were directionally the more correct half of the respondents, and low on the 50 percent number. "Our industry is driven by 'what's new' so we are constantly creating new products," was the response of one consumer-product executive in the Wharton/George Group survey.

Two years ago when I queried several companies I know well and believe are well managed, there was a prolonged delay in response when I first asked questions about how much their offerings had grown. This was followed a few days—or a few weeks—later by information, and the admission that all were surprised at how many new offerings they had added. Even then, responses that are round numbers like 1,500 or 3,000 were still likely estimates. It is rare that an actual count of SKUs comes out to a nice round number. The companies that had a working SKU tracking system made responses like 1,766 or 18,221.

A Simple Example—One White Coffee Mug

Take the simple white coffee mug, and assume that it is your product. If you have one style, one color, one size, in one package, sourced from one supplier, packaged and stocked in one location, you can accurately compute a standard cost of $1.00 for your mug in terms of material, labor, and overhead (the old way) or material plus cost of acquisition plus fixed and variable conversion costs (a newer way).

Expand your coffee mug line to 4 styles, 8 colors, 2 sizes, and 6 package variations sourced from a total of 5 suppliers and packaged upon receipt at the 2 distribution centers. There are now at least 384 mug SKUs to be stocked in 2 locations. Mathematically, from the potential mixtures of colors, sizes, package variations, and special assortments, the number of possible combinations quickly becomes astronomical (theoretically, 2.7 with 17 zeroes). Even if such an incredible array is not actually created, this example illustrates the potential for explosive complexity of a magnitude that is surprising. Each unique combination then requires an item number, packaging/labels, processing documentation, tooling, new inventory SKUs, etc. The "standard cost" of an individual packaged mug or one of a set of mugs would still be almost the same as before at $1.00/mug, or at least very close to that.

But something is wrong. Intuitively, you now know that somehow there are many hidden costs that the cost system doesn't measure. Even if all the color variations of a mug cost nearly the same (a reasonable assumption) and there is only a small incremental difference in packaging costs (also a reasonable assumption), the cost of the mug remains almost unchanged. Do you think the cost of selling and supplying the mug is unchanged? Not a chance. But where do those costs show up?

The possible combinations and permutations on orders have grown dramatically, and that's before any ripple effects on marketing's collateral materials, purchasing (more items to create, maintain, document, package, and buy), and forecast volatility (more customers and more SKUs to forecast). That's before marketing starts mixing models in merchandising assortments that vary by market, customer, and production/DC location. After all this, the standard cost of the mugs remained largely unchanged, and given a constant price assumption, so does the profitability. Right? No! Wrong!

The costs associated with this sort of complexity will be buried in accounting classifications that are non-product-specific. Variances will grow. Inventory levels and obsolescence will increase. Fixed overhead and administrative-staff costs will grow to handle the complexity, but little of this will be attributed to the real causes. And because the information comes in at the end of accounting periods, the cause-and-effect relationships will have become obscured by time. The profits are gone, value destroyed, and the evidence of the crime is circumstantial at best. The suspects are few, the accomplices many, and the guilty are almost impossible to find. Now you have a small taste of the Complexity Crisis at work.

Manage in Real Time: Define the Problem Clearly, Then Fix It Fast!

Today's information and data-gathering technology makes it possible to determine the results of a business each day. There is no reason to wait until a calendar month end to learn whether your company is making or losing money. All that does is give complexity more time to eat away at the profitability. It is time to change behaviors from old-fashioned, outdated ones, which arose from the slow, manual accumulation of data. Now you can—and should—strive to manage with near real-time information. Solving problems is so much easier if you can "catch the culprits in the act" and take remedial action on the spot. Don't ask "why can't we do that," because people will answer your question and tell you why you can't. Ask "how can we" and start solving complexity-related waste faster and faster.

The other reason complexity is such a vexing problem is that it goes unrecognized as a root cause of so many other problems. When a company's overhead or SG&A climbs faster than revenue for no apparent reason except that it takes more people to get the work done, there is a very high likelihood that growing complexity is one of the primary causes. If inventory turns drop while obsolete and noncurrent inventory increases, you can bet that is a symptom of growing complexity. When customer service just can't keep up and there is no immediately obvious cause, look for complexity as a factor, if not the primary cause. If variances increase in rework, repacking, premium freight charges (like airfreight), or heavy use of services like FedEx or UPS Next Day in your domestic market, a prime suspect might be complexity. When the intellectual property managers, the tax managers, the internal-audit staff, and public accounting firms all encounter higher costs for staffing, travel, and administration, complexity should be a primary suspect.

The longer you let these problems accumulate and wait for month-end or quarter-end results to begin solving them, the more of your precious time and money complexity-based problems will have consumed. When more products are being created, maintained, and sold to more customers, using more components from more suppliers and doing business in more countries or markets—or any combination of these factors—complexity is driving up the costs of the business.

Because growth-driven complexity usually means new products being sold to new customers in new places, there is little basis for accurate forecasts. Forecasts will be wrong, which results in poor service, too much inventory, too many of the wrong items, and too few of the right items. While inventories rise, customer service falls. Obsolete and noncurrent inventory grows and customer service is overloaded with inquiries about when their goods are coming, or why they aren't already there. New products being sold in new countries also test the quality of the intellectual-property protection; new legal entities require new reporting and tax returns, etc. Internal-audit staff still must worry about the controls in domestic operations and now it must audit new, faraway places staffed with new people, doing new transactions.

Measure It and Keep Measuring It

There are several appropriate clichés that can be cited here. "What gets measured gets done," and "If you can't measure it, you can't manage it." There are more, but these two will suffice to convey the message. While they are overused, they are also largely true, which is why they are used so often. Management operates by focusing on exceptions. Like driving a car or flying a plane, when every gauge is in the right place and no warning lights are flashing, the assumption is that everything is operating A-OK. If the measurements—management's gauges and warning lights—aren't monitoring the right things, no alarms will be going off until the period-end financial statements reveal the carnage. In too many businesses, by the time a given month's financial statements are circulated and analyzed, the next month is about one-third over. That means even when problem-solving steps are taken quickly, a second month will suffer from the same problems, and that means two-thirds of the quarter's results will be adversely impacted. Thus, it's key to use the right new metrics and use them vigilantly.

Another time-proven cliché is that "an ounce of prevention is worth a pound of cure." That means it is important to focus on measurements that can be used prospectively instead of retrospectively. If the metrics can be designed to be used in advance of decisions, there will be much less need for damage control when the remaining metrics set off warnings.

Build Your Strategy: Find It, Fix It, Then Use It or Lose It—But Don't Confuse It

This is the point where you reach the proverbial fork in the road. As the legendary pitcher Satchel Paige once said, "If you don't know where you're headed, any road will take you there." Decisions can be changed if circumstances change or new knowledge/information becomes available. That said, decisions must be made to get things moving, and then action must be taken, or nothing will change.

If you suspect that complexity is a problem and not an advantage, then it is time to find that complexity and fix it—which means drive it out of the business. On the other hand, if a high-variety, complexity-rich solution appears to yield competitive advantage, it is time to determine how the structure, processes, and culture/relationships of the company must be altered to execute such a strategy profitably.

Customers are often willing to pay more for customized solutions. This is a clue to an opportunity to compete with complexity. Alternatively, your company may be better equipped to systematically offer greater complexity at a lower relative cost than competitors, and thus create a differentiable competitive advantage. If the market is headed toward commoditization, the choice must be made whether to drive to a low-cost strategy and eliminate complexity in the process or to drive toward an innovation strategy built around new and more varied options. This is a key strategic decision, and one that requires a good understanding of customer needs and market-competitive dynamics as well as your company's ability to successfully adapt. Don't make this decision lightly. Also, once you have decided, don't become confused about whether your direction will be to use complexity or to remove it. Make a plan, communicate it, and then execute it.

If You Want to Lose It—Declare War on Complexity, Like Motorola Did

When Theresa Metty arrived at Motorola from IBM sometime in 2001, she found that Motorola had been late to recognize the switch from analog to digital mobile phones and, as a result, lost market share to Nokia. In its efforts to catch up, it made a common mistake. I call it the "throwing things at the wall to see what sticks" approach to innovation. In doing this, you generate a lot of new product ideas and push them rapidly into the market. The result is usually proliferation and complexity of epic proportions.

Motorola was no exception. It had created complexity that was adversely impacting everything. Metty and her organization found that Motorola had three times as many design platforms, three or four times as many models (65+) and twice the number of unique parts as was needed. In simpler terms, Motorola was at least two and perhaps as much as four times as complex as its competitors. In a speaking presentation, Metty outlined the problems, the approach, and some results of what she termed Motorola's "War on Complexity." Subsequent articles chronicled its progress and the huge benefits to Motorola.

The "Complexity Poster Child" in Metty's presentation was one particular cell phone with:

- Over 100 different factory configurations
- Four housing colors
- Thirty software versions
- No software postponement
- No hardware postponement
- Nonstandard IC, display, battery
- Lead-time of four-plus weeks for components from suppliers

Clearly this was a forecasting and production nightmare. Imagine 100 different phones, each with 100 different configurations in multiple colors, with different batteries, and so on. What are the odds on getting the right ones built? Almost zero. The result of this kind of runaway proliferation is inflated inventories, poor customer service, and excessive costs in both purchasing and production.

The solution Motorola chose was fewer products, less complex products, more standard-parts usage, more reuse of products from other phones, and more use of postponement to add different features at the latest possible time.

Thus, Motorola's War On Complexity was declared—to address both its portfolio complexity and its product complexity—the "two-headed monster," as Metty called it.

Motorola's approach to defining the two-headed monster went like this:

At a Portfolio Level

- Too many products
- Too many high-complexity products
- Too many low-volume models

At a Detail Level

- Not enough component reuse
- Too many nonstandard parts
- Too little use of postponement
- Too many models
- Too many parts
- Too complex subassemblies

The Complexity Index

The preceding lists reveal that opportunities to reduce Motorola's complexity existed in standardization, in reuse of standard items, in postponement, and in improved design for both manufacture and modularity. To control this process, and monitor complexity in new designs, Motorola created a proprietary "Complexity Index" (CI). This was a mathematical representation of ten factors in the cell phone's design that, taken in the aggregate, yielded a numerical result. While the computation was proprietary, many of the factors were revealed later. Here are seven of the ten:

1. Average part count
2. Test time
3. Assembly time
4. Mechanical postponement
5. Software postponement
6. Use of industry-standard parts
7. Component reuse

Knowing all ten factors is not that important, nor is the exact computation used in arriving at the Complexity Index, because each product and/or industry requires a unique list of factors. For simplicity's sake, the math Motorola used yielded an index of 1 for best in class. Lower than 1 was better than the prior best in class and higher than 1 meant inferior to the best. An index of more than 1 usually required a redesign of the product before its release to production and procurement.

This sounds very simple and straightforward—until you consider that such a process demands behavioral change from thousands of employees and hundreds of suppliers scattered around the globe. Getting them to rally around the War on Complexity was no simple task. First the senior levels of management had to buy in and support the effort—visibly. This process involved business-sector presidents actually assembling phones and seeing the issues. Then came the massive communications effort, ranging from town-hall meetings to global broadcasts via electronic media.

The problem was that most employees couldn't see the full complexity picture. This is a common and difficult challenge in the Complexity Crisis. Complexity results from a huge number of decisions—some large and many small—that occur constantly throughout an organization. The larger and more widespread the organization is, the more difficult it is to get everyone on the same page in seeing and addressing such a problem and the necessary solutions. To give you an idea of the sheer magnitude of Motorola's problem at that time, consider this: it had 145 batteries, 78 displays, and 1,447 software versions!

Whenever an organization is asked to change how they do things, there is resistance to change from the people. Some of the resistance comes from the normal personal reactions: "What does this mean to me?" "What's in it for me?" "Why change; things are working okay now?" To overcome such resistance to change, the need and reasons for change must be personalized—translated so that they answer those questions—and more like them. The following is an example of how Motorola tried to make it personal:

PERSONALIZE IT—MAKE IT RELEVANT TO PEOPLE BY TYING IT TO THEIR SUCCESS

- To a salesperson, low complexity means delighted customers, shorter lead-times, and a responsive and cost-effective supply chain
- To a finance person, low complexity means lower product costs, less inventory, improved cash flow, and less excess and obsolescence
- To a product-development person, low complexity means shorter development-cycle times, less parts to qualify, and fewer suppliers

Motorola's solutions might not work exactly for you and your situation, but they are so fundamentally sound that it is worth considering how parts of them can be adapted to other situations. Obviously, the development of something like a Complexity Index (CI) is a company- and product-specific (or service-) matter. Different aspects of product/service designs add complexity and others add value depending on the product or service involved. Addressing these aspects of complexity up front is the right way to proceed. This CI concept is also a good one because it sets an impersonal but agreed-upon criteria for a design to meet. Create a test metric. Call it a Complexity Index if you want, one that rolls multiple design factors into one measurement. Use the CI as a gatekeeper to disqualify overly complex designs and send them back to the drawing board.

Portfolios, Platforms, and Teams with Leaders and Champions

Once the concept of reducing complexity is broadly communicated and accepted, there is much work to do. A key element is to understand product portfolios. Explaining this concept thoroughly is beyond the scope of this book. I will only say here that portfolio management requires an in-depth understanding of what customers (and end-users/consumers) believe is important and valuable and also how competitors attempt to achieve that end, in comparison to your approach. Portfolios consider market segments served, price-value relationships, and the allocation of resources to achieve the desired goals. Obviously, complexity can have a dramatic adverse impact on a portfolio, its plans, and outcomes. In their book *Conquering Complexity in Your Business,* Michael George and Stephen Wilson state that "portfolio and process complexity is often a larger drag on profits and growth than any other single factor in a business."

Another important step is to understand the use of product platforms as a way to reduce complexity—and that is a key part of coping with the Complexity Crisis. A platform is the common design structure upon which varied components—hardware, software, practices, etc.—are added to create customer-desired unique variations.

Let's take a very simple example—an ice cream sundae. The platform is the dish and the scoop size. Variations are ice cream flavors, topping flavors, and final toppings (nuts, whipped cream, cherry, etc.). While this example is admittedly simplistic, it is a case of platform design in which postponement is used to provide a very high variety of consumer-desired outcomes with a relatively low variety of standardized components.

During Chrysler's resurgence of the 1990s, it used platforms and configuration changes very successfully. It created families of products around platforms, which allowed it to introduce new cars faster and use production facilities and parts more flexibly than its domestic U.S. competitors, Ford and GM. Unfortunately, most of the key architects of that strategy left before or during the 1998 acquisition of Chrysler by Daimler.

The teams who participate in actual product and component platforms require leaders, and individual areas also require champions, since this approach requires behavioral modification both internally and externally. Thus, it takes someone who will pursue the goals with the passion of a champion to assure success. Conquering complexity requires much more than business as usual.

Another key element of using a gatekeeper metric such as a Complexity Index is for everyone to understand that designs and projects do not move to the next stage of development unless they pass complexity tests. This concept can be used both internally and with suppliers. Early involvement of suppliers was another fundamental that Motorola used in its War on Complexity. This is always good business practice, but it is even more important in defeating complexity. The earlier key suppliers can be involved in new product projects, the more valuable their input can be. This type of partnership behavior is one of the central messages of my earlier books. Suppliers can also help reinforce the use of industry-standard components where possible, reserving the complexity of unique components to where they create unique competitive advantages.

FIKIF—Fix It; Keep It Fixed

Complexity piles up over time like cobwebs in a dusty corner. When the right behaviors for the recognition and containment of complexity have been institutionalized, these cobwebs get noticed and knocked down. There is also much less likelihood of a relapse creating new complexity. Since sales and marketing are always seeking new products, and proliferation via line extensions and derivative products are tempting and easy, constant vigilance is needed. Complexity creeps back in like a thief in the night, leaving only the evidence that something valuable is missing—hard-earned profits.

To reinforce the benefits of declaring a war on complexity as Motorola did, consider these results after less than two years:

MOTOROLA'S WAR ON COMPLEXITY—THE RESULTS

- Removed $2.6 billion in supply-chain costs
- Reduced inventory by $1.3 billion
- Reduced supply-chain employment by 12,500
- Closed five manufacturing sites that were no longer needed
- Improved on-time delivery by 48 percent
- Reduced product complexity by 23 percent

(*Note:* Motorola's mobile business was $10–$12 billion in annual sales in this period.)

If You Want To Use It, Match Your Execution to Your Strategy—Like Dell

The Dell Computer story is well known. The company decided that the only way to compete in a market where its material prices were constantly dropping was to wait until the last possible moment to purchase and configure the computer that used those components. Considering the huge variety of potential configurations a consumer might buy and guessing at the mix of models and features was a futile exercise. Dell simply decided to enable the consumer to go online or on the phone to configure and order their own unique computer. Then, Dell would assemble and ship it within a few days.

By developing this form of business model, Dell was able to use complexity as a competitive tool, beating competitors (IBM, HP/ Compaq, Gateway, and others) who had to guess at what configurations consumers wanted, then make the computers, distribute them to retail outlets, and hope they sold before prices dropped still further.

During discussions with a former Compaq top executive who was there during Dell's growth spurt, he confirmed how Dell beat Compaq:

> They'd [Dell] just make whatever the consumer wanted but for corporate clients, they also figured out the best combinations of features to bundle and could deliver these fast and complete. Meanwhile, we [Compaq] had this huge list of models and options. The corporate customers would choose a few of this and a few of that, and when they were done choosing, there were always a few small items we were out of, so we couldn't make one or two models and couldn't ship the complete order on time.

History has proven that Dell capitalized on complexity wisely to win in this stage of the computer-market wars. The question now is, has commoditization of PCs progressed so far that losing complexity may be Dell's best new strategy? And what does that mean to the Dell business model? Why has it not proven nearly as effective in recent years as it expanded into servers, printers, routers, and consumer electronics? Wall Street is asking these same questions, which is one reason Dell's stock has faltered, and Michael Dell has reclaimed the top spot. His challenge now will be how to build on past success without introducing crippling complexity into the business as he does so.

It appears that the plateau in computer pricing, the shift by consumers to laptops, and the failure of Dell's current strategy to adapt to consumer changes are all partially to blame. Dell, which was sensitive to consumers direct ordering via 800 lines or the Internet, appears to have been equally insensitive to consumer trends, and this has given HP (Compaq's new parent) a new advantage—a dominant position at retail—one that Dell is ill-equipped to challenge.

There are several certainties about complexity and consumers. Complexity creates waste, and excessive choice turns off consumers, but ignoring consumers' wants and wishes can be the most damaging error of all. If consumers want (and will pay for) complexity, then sell it to them; if consumers want simplicity and instant gratification, cut out the complexity and sell the simple, speedy solution instead.

Don't Get Stuck in the Middle

There is a great temptation to rationalize the wisdom of staying where you are, even if it is the wrong place. If your business is one that should be cutting complexity and isn't, beware of the temptation to suggest that you can compete on complexity. Matt Reilly, senior vice president of client services at the George Group, puts it well: "Using product proliferation as a strategy very frequently does not create value, and often destroys value even as it produces revenue."

Remember the earlier chapter describing the income statement, where the top line goes up and the bottom line goes down, and everyone is perplexed about this outcome? That is the unrecognized effect of complexity on many areas of the business. First, identify the problems—and measure them. Second, begin solving them—install the fixes, and make sure they stay fixed.

I'd like to close this chapter with another, more difficult TAC in the form of a riddle. You may have to think hard about this one, as there is a trick in it.

TAC #4: THE TWO-MILE DRIVE

A man must drive two miles and average 60 miles per hour for the trip. He decides to drive the first mile at 30 miles per hour. How fast must he drive the second mile to reach his two-mile destination and average 60 miles per hour?

Think about this one a bit longer. Have you figured it out yet? If you said his task is now impossible, you are right. When he decided to drive 30 mph for the first mile, he used two minutes. Since 60 mph is a mile per minute, the only way to average 60 mph is for him to complete the two-mile trip in two minutes, but he already used the two minutes because he decided to go too slowly on the first half of the trip. This is a common error in business. According to Peter Drucker, "Time is the scarcest resource and unless it is managed nothing else can be managed." Failing to make timely decisions and then taking prompt action can ultimately reduce or (as in the riddle) completely eliminate your chance of success.

Time is the one perishable asset that neither money nor effort can replace once it is gone. If your business is suffering from complexity, time is precious. Don't waste time now, because you might not be able to get where you need to go, in time, later on.

HOW TO RECOGNIZE IT, MEASURE IT, AND BEGIN TO FIX IT

Remember: You Can't Manage What You Can't Measure

> *"Willingness to change is a strength, even if it means plunging part of the company into total confusion for a while."*
>
> —Jack Welch, former chairman and CEO, General Electric

Few parts of a business are so underestimated and poorly measured as complexity. None of the accounting systems used to measure the financial success of a business is designed to capture the costs of complexity or the penalties of proliferation. Just think about the hypothetical situation in the examples of the P and L or the simple coffee mug. There are more products, selling to more customers, made from more components, coming from more places, being produced and distributed in more locations than ever before. But, is all of this complexity actually adding to the company's profitability? Unless this is an exceptional case, the answer is no.

Managers and executives striving to achieve more-demanding growth goals add this complexity voluntarily, and often, unconsciously. Whole departments—R & D, Product Development, Marketing, Sales—work to innovate and create new products, sell to new customers, and open new channels of distribution, all in hopes of achieving elusive growth targets. The more difficult or slower growing the market, the harder they push and the more complexity they create. The problem of complexity that plagues today's businesses, managers, and executives is an insidious result of their own actions. Like a modern-day Dr. Frankenstein, with the best of intentions, they have created the monster. It lurks in many parts of the business, unmeasured, while draining resources, focus, and energy. Now it is time to expose it, learn to both measure and control it, and then decide whether to lose it or use it—specifically, reduce it by driving out complexity or develop a strategy to compete based on complexity, with the structure and processes to do just that.

TAC #5: THERE ARE ONLY FIVE WAYS TO GROW FASTER THAN THE MARKET IS GROWING

1. Take share from existing competitors.

2. Expand the market with innovative new offerings.

3. Change the mix to sell higher-price-value products.

4. Enter new market segments or an entirely new market (go back to numbers 1–3 of this list).

5. Create an entirely new product and market (e.g., FedEx package delivery, bagged chopped lettuce, or eBay online auctions).

Growth—Only Five Choices

Let's briefly examine each of the choices in the TAC for pros and cons.

First, and most obvious, is trying to take market share from competitors, as it involves participation in the same markets, competing with familiar competitors, products, etc. Choosing this path to growth usually doesn't add complexity unless the share you go after is a different kind of product, customer, distribution, etc. Then it can be doubly difficult, since there will be the dual risk of entering quasi-new markets with less-familiar products, battling it out on pricing and deals, and still adding complexity in the process. This approach is also one of the most difficult from the perspective of profitability and likely competitive retaliation. You fight for their share, and get some—at a cost—and they come right back after a piece of yours. This is not pretty. It's tough.

The second choice, expanding the market through innovation, sounds great. It's just much easier to say than to do. Innovations are not too predictable and are subject to copying, knockoffs, or product life-cycle limitations. Good ones can be very powerful, but for every few that work, many will fail. Or, they'll cannibalize older, existing products/services. This is also an attractive trap. New products, new customers, new markets, etc. all lead to new complexity, which won't be apparent in the financial projections, but it will show in the financial results.

The third option, changing the mix, is a very effective way to impact profitability and would be a great solution for growth—if everyone else wasn't also trying to do the same thing. Still, it is important to analyze the relative profitability of the products and customers, and to evaluate if you can shift the mix from the less-profitable to more-profitable customers or products and from lower-growth to higher-growth product or market segments. This is also a strategy that is less likely to cause more complexity and might actually lead to simpler product and customer combinations.

The fourth choice has appeal because the grass is always greener on the other side of the fence. New markets look so attractive because we aren't as familiar with them. Remember, however, that while new markets may be new to you, they are some incumbent's current market, and that incumbent will defend its market position. What you will do is add a huge number of "news"—products, specs, customers, locations, etc.—all of which will add hidden complexity and the costs associated with it.

Finally, the fifth option is a wonderful one. It is also the most difficult and uncertain, and contains elements of the prior four. FedEx created a whole new market, but its core business of delivering packages and "information in packets" was previously done by mail, freight, fax, phone, etc. And each of these market segments had entrenched incumbents defending its turf in one way or another.

One of the most interesting new market-growth efforts was created by the realization that time-starved U.S. consumers would pay handsomely for the convenience of buying bagged, chopped lettuce. This created a new, multi-billion-dollar market. This kind of a breakthrough is rare.

The more innovative the new entrant—like eBay—the more immediately successful it can be versus less desirable, older ways (newspaper classified ads, yard sales, thrift stores, etc.). The more advantages the new method offers (like the ability to use digital photos on eBay to show products), the more likely it is to displace the older method. But remember, eBay built itself on three big new technological advances:

widespread access to the Internet, wide acceptance of digital photography, and cashless payment systems (PayPal, and others).

These great new growth successes look so obvious now, but each had its own risks of complexity and hidden costs of doing unfamiliar things in unfamiliar ways.

Bottom line: achieving profitable growth is difficult without creating and managing new complexity. Finally, these challenges of growth are being recognized more widely. Managing complexity before the resultant problems cause a crisis is imperative. That's why this is called the Complexity *Crisis*. Consider these thoughts from "Innovation vs. Complexity—What is too much of a good thing?" a 2005 *Harvard Business Review* article. The authors, Mark Gottfredson and Keith Aspinall, consider the appropriate balance between innovation and complexity. "But the pursuit of innovation can be taken too far. As a company increases the pace of innovation, its profitability often begins to stagnate or even erode. The reason can be summed up in one word: complexity. The continual launch of new products and line extensions adds complexity throughout a company's operations, and, as the costs of managing that complexity multiply, margins shrink." Innovation-driven sales growth is the reward for success. Failure creates problems of complexity with its hidden costs. The study confirms this fact.

Mark Gottfredson and Keith Aspinall continue, "Managers aren't blind to the problem. Nearly 70 percent admit that excessive complexity is raising their costs and hindering profit growth, according to a 2005 Bain survey of more than 900 global executives. What managers often miss is the true source of the problem—the way complexity begins in the product line and then spreads outward through every facet of a company's operations."

Few companies properly count and track the exploding number of products, customers, markets, variations, facilities, people, suppliers, etc., which lead to an even greater explosion of part numbers, processes, bills of materials, invoices, payments, entries, transactions, lenders, legal entities, countries/cultures, currencies, etc. The list of how complexity spreads is almost endless. As financial pressures mount, finding new markets and new products with which to grow is a daunting task. Doing so without dramatically increasing complexity is even harder. Yet, innovation is essential; but it must be managed innovation, not simply rampant proliferation.

Innovation Versus Complexity—Do Costs Rise Faster Than Revenues?

The old, standard cost systems measured material costs to four decimal places. Industrial engineers and efficiency experts parsed down labor costs to tiny fractions of an hour, using lean production to wring waste out of each and every task and process. Accountants and purchasing managers hammer down the costs of services, expenses, overheads, and indirect costs. However, no one is responsible for finding complexity and reducing it.

Of course, there are periodic facility and product-line rationalizations, but larger economic forces usually drive these. All of the talent and attention is focused on actions that add complexity, and few or none on those that reduce it. Peter Drucker would applaud devoting the best talent to pursuit of the greatest opportunities. He would also caution that there must still be attention given to cleaning up and discontinuing the "misses" and products that have outlived their useful lives. When the scarce resources of people, time, and money are spread over more and more items, more relationships, and more landscapes, something has to give, and it usually does. People drown in complexity-induced work and are pressed for time, and deadlines must be extended to do the extra work. Finally, profit is reduced by complexity's many hidden cost impacts.

As Barry Schwartz notes in his book, *The Paradox of Choice*, studies have proven that too much variety actually results in lower sales. Consumers become confused and don't buy. The reason for the proliferation—increased sales—actually inhibits prospective buyers by adding *too many* choices and is also a major cause of the Complexity Crisis. What a paradoxical outcome—a self-defeating growth initiative.

ADDING COMPLEXITY IS EASY

> When Bain and Company studied the complexity issue, its findings reinforced every aspect of the previous conclusion: "It's natural for businesses to add products to keep customers happy. Smart marketers have no trouble justifying each addition as a means of adding or protecting revenue. But as more products are added, the costs of the resulting complexity begin to outweigh the revenues—and profits start falling. From that point on, every new offering—however attractive in isolation—just thins margins further. The more aggressively the company innovates in product development, the weaker its results become. ...What makes the problem particularly damaging is that it tends to be invisible to management."

Does this mean you shouldn't innovate? Of course not. Does it mean you should curtail new product development? Maybe, maybe not. What it means is that you need to understand what is happening and create awareness and visibility of complexity at work. Once that has been done, solutions emerge, many of which have been amply tested with results that are almost astonishingly good.

Understand Warning Signs—Look for Symptoms

The story about Theresa Metty coming to Motorola from IBM as head of its supply chain management, and finding a mess, is one that could be retold many times over, at many other companies. Motorola's plight was not that different. What happened to cause Motorola's problems was the same set of events that happens time and again. Are they happening at your company or one that you work with—a supplier or customer? Metty's remarks in a 2001 interview in *Purchasing* magazine listed the breadth and depth of the issues and gave some clues to how she planned to attack complexity.

"I couldn't find anybody who thought buying industry standard components was important."

"There wasn't a lot of concern about reusing components."

"You could afford to start from scratch every time you designed a new phone."

"We found ourselves with tens of thousands of different part numbers from numerous suppliers."

She assembled a combination of ideas into a coherent set of solutions for Motorola and, over the next few years, achieved a tremendous amount of savings, supply chain streamlining, and strategic sourcing, without sacrificing Motorola's competitive product position one iota. The essence of her idea is summarized in this one statement from her 2001 interview, something confirmed by a later conversation I had with her:

"We have rallied around this concept of reduced complexity. We don't want to make phones any more complex than is necessary. In addition, when the phone has to be unique, we want to design it so the differentiation can be added at the last possible moment. That lets you be responsive because you can build the generic model to a certain point and then add the differentiation. It will help keep inventories down, too."

Many of the solutions adopted at Motorola in its War on Complexity were not new—but the combination to defeat complexity *was* a new solution set. Most of these time-proven disciplines had been forgotten or overlooked in the scramble to chase new products and regain lost market position.

Platforms, Teams, and Platform Commodity Councils

Create "platforms" around which products can be built with variations, making it unnecessary to completely redesign the product to meet different market segment needs. Once the platforms are defined, then other means of simplification can be tested for applicability.

Standard Component Lists

We used these when I worked for GTE in telecommunications design. Standardization was critical since telephone equipment needed to be very reliable, thus the standard components had to be ultrareliable. Having standard spare parts was also crucial.

Approved Supplier Lists

This is a throwback to the era of standardization, but because an idea worked once before doesn't mean it won't work as well again. Standard component lists allows sourcing to shop for the best deals, but within a group of approved suppliers known to provide reliable service and dependable quality. Suppliers can now be either ten miles or ten thousand miles away. This alters the decisions about the number and location of "approved suppliers." Another by-product of using approved suppliers is that it enhances quality, because suppliers can be certified and engaged in longer-term plans for the development of new products. Using fewer suppliers automatically reduces variability.

Long-term Agreements and Road Maps

By carefully vetting suppliers and limiting the number of suppliers and components, there is another advantage that emerges. Long-term contracts can be negotiated, creating greater stability and lessening complexity in supply chain relationships. This can also lead to earlier supplier involvement in new-product development, which accelerates the time to market for new products and provides a better overall design by incorporating supplier know-how into the design process.

Postponement

The term "postponement" describes using common platforms and adding differentiated features and cosmetics (and custom packaging) as close to final demand as possible. By holding components in a semi-finished condition, much of the complexity otherwise introduced by model-to-model variations can be greatly reduced. This has become a common practice in many industries, particularly the technology segments, where it is used in connection with "mass customization."

Mass Customization

Related to postponement is a concept called "mass customization," coming from a book of the same name by B. Joseph Pine. Mass customization describes the process in which mass-production techniques are used until the product reaches a nearly finished state, and the differentiators that customize the product are added at the latest possible time. Computer-printer makers such as HP and Lexmark use common platforms, postponement, and mass customization to create a wide variety of models without driving up complexity.

A Complexity Index

The term Complexity Index, described earlier, was coined by Theresa Metty and her associates at Motorola to describe the gatekeeper tool for screening new product designs to prevent unnecessary and costly complexity. A Complexity Index can use weighting to denote the relative importance of the various factors in its makeup and to arrive at a single numerical index. Remember just two benefits of Motorola's War on Complexity: savings of $2.6 billion and inventory reduction of $1.3 billion with improved service levels. Complexity can be a big issue, but when there is an all-out war declared on complexity, the rewards can also be big.

Too Many Options—A New Solution

The following story and the solution it describes started in the early 1990s at the Georgia Institute of Technology, when an automotive OEM (original equipment manufacturer) conferred with industrial and systems engineering professor Roy Marsten. The question posed was, "How can we determine the right number and the right set of configurations for our electrical components?" The specific component was an under-dash wiring harness for a vehicle. This harness might contain the wires that control as many as twenty options ranging from seats to mirrors, radios to lighting. If only fifteen of these options were used in varying combinations, the number of possible harnesses was 32,768. Now there is complexity at work.

Because of current needs, the OEM already had 100 different harnesses, but knew intuitively that this complexity would get worse before it got better if it didn't do something differently. Dr. Marsten used his years of experience in computational optimization to build a mathematical model to represent product configurations and developed the first set of algorithms to address the problems of too many product configurations. No one knew what the profitability was for each potential configuration. Nor did they know how to find the optimal set of configurations while minimizing costs (and maximizing profits).

Roy Marsten founded Emcien in 2001. I learned about its work a year later, and I discussed it with the company CEO, Radhika Subramanian. She related a few examples of how their work had been progressing, and I knew immediately that Emcien's solutions were important and deserved a mention in the Complexity Crisis. Whereas most of the solutions I offer are simple, straightforward, and easy to implement, some problems just don't yield to those kinds of solutions. Some problems are just too complex to wrap your mind around, and you need the help of a computer with programs developed by specialists like Emcien.

Emcien Created a New Category of Configuration Analytics

Many companies suffer from the growing problem of product line proliferation and a continuous explosion of product configurations. More and more options on more and more products seem necessary to serve market demands. The cost of providing this wide variety of products and options reduces profitability and slows response to customer needs. Emcien developed a new category of analytical applications directed squarely at solving this type of problem. They call it Product Mix Management (PMM). PMM uses technology to support the decision-making process by analyzing customer demand with visualization, shaping, and trend techniques, as well as complex analyses for optimizing product-line decisions, which many companies do with "gut feel" and guesswork.

For example, companies know that many added configurations increase total supply chain and design costs, and they realize it must be a significant cost. The insightful ones also wonder which configurations are profitable and which are not. While they don't know how to go about solving this kind of complexity problem, it will be encouraging for them to know there is now a solution out there. With solutions like Emcien's, it is possible to optimize—to consolidate offerings, to minimize the cost of complexity and still satisfy a wide range of customer needs.

Sales must serve a wide variety of customer needs to compete; product engineering gets overloaded as product variations expand. Procurement has to manage more, different components for more models than ever and demand forecasting at the item level becomes far more error prone. Production is at the tail end of the process, thus it must cope with frequent changeovers and demands. Logistics must handle more SKUs with less lead time and make sure the service hits the right product-delivery window. Customer service still needs the right inventory and product information, while everyone must deal with the explosion of complexity.

This parallels the sequence of events that I've been describing over and over—just with a much greater level of mathematical complexity. This is the kind of complexity challenge that doesn't yield to simple solutions. That requires powerful, computer-based systems like Emcien's, to analyze, manage and optimize all levels of the product line, including platforms and components. Its systems consider materials costs and supply chain costs balanced against forecast demand and potential revenues/profits for each of the configurations. The programs do this for different groupings and show risk, revenue, and profit by configuration. This is invaluable in analyzing which combinations of configurations yield the most profitable overall product mix.

Emcien also offers the ability to plan at a configuration level, not just in aggregate. Most systems take a collective view for planning, but execution must always consider each SKU. The system provides simulation, optimization, and prediction information for product line decisions. I've taken this amount of space to describe one particular solution (Emcien's) because I believe it is conceptually a leading-edge approach to quantifying large-scale complexity. Computers are not necessarily the solution to many complexity-related problems, but some problems just naturally yield to computer-based analysis better than others. The challenge is to use the right tool for the given situation, and reduce complexity, not add more of it.

AN EXAMPLE—A MINIVAN MANUFACTURER

When a manufacturer designs a new vehicle, one of the essential parts is the instrument-panel wiring harness (IPWH), because it contains wires that feed information both from and to many different parts of the vehicle. The challenge is to decide how many different kinds of wiring harnesses to make. Too many configurations reduce the volume of each one for production and multiply the risk of having the wrong inventory, which can jeopardize production. Putting all the wires into one IPWH means wasting money on unused wires and the labor to include them, since only a few of the vehicles use all the possible options.

In one case, there were twenty-seven different options that the minivan harness had to accommodate. The challenge was to optimize how many different IPWHs to use to cover the 7 million potential variations in possible configurations. Obviously, the relative popularity of various options was a major consideration in this complexity challenge. Using the manufacturer's information about the cost of the components installed but not used, it was determined that about $50 was wasted content. Analysis of demand and cost data was fed into Emcien's optimizer and a solution for every number of harnesses from 3 to 10 was developed. This range was chosen based on management estimates and prior practice.

The final solution led to nine different harnesses and yielded a savings of about $10 per IPWH over prior practice, which translated into an annual savings of $2.5 million by eliminating the wasted use of 2.4 million components in the minivan's IPWH.

Some complexity problems require more robust or rigorous solutions. Such solution tools exist and are being used by leading companies. You can see other examples of how computer-based analysis can help eliminate waste due to complexity at *www.emcien.com.*

A NEW METRIC FOR TRACKING COMPLEXITY

Figuring Out the Complexity Factor
for Your Business

"All generalizations are false, including this one."
—Mark Twain

How did the problem of complexity go unnoticed until it reached epidemic proportions? The answer is both simple and complex. Nobody measured it—at least not completely. Parts of the causes and effects of complexity were measured, some quite widely. But businesses must compete in more, different, and increasingly complex markets than ever before. This adds many dimensions to problems caused by complexity, and also defies simple metrics.

This chapter will cover how to use several measures to track complexity. Much like checking your blood pressure, temperature, and pulse, those factors in and of themselves don't tell the doctor exactly what's wrong with you. However, these diagnostics do tell the doctor if something might be wrong and point to what/where that might be. Combine these tests with other diagnostic tools and measurements and an entire illness can be more clearly understood. Then the time comes to decide how to deal with complexity strategically—whether to use it or lose it—and such procedures will help guide the decision on how to proceed. They will also ensure, regardless of whatever decision is made for dealing with complexity, that they can be checked from time to time, and that the approach doesn't waver at the first sign of new market pressures.

Rank Factors in Descending Order

One of the most useful management tools, especially in understanding where a company makes money and where it loses money, is the descending-order list. Rank customers by annual sales from highest to lowest. Calculate the percentage each customer contributes to total sales and then create a cumulative percentage column. This column will help you do a Pareto (80–20) analysis.

PARETO'S PRINCIPLE—
THE 80/20 RULE

Vilfredo Pareto was a nineteenth-century Italian economist who discovered what is now known as the Pareto Principle or "80–20 rule." Pareto first recognized the principle, when he realized that 80 percent of the land in Italy was owned by 20 percent of the population. Later, he discovered that the principle was valid in many other situations, including gardening, where 80 percent of his garden peas were produced by 20 percent of the peapods. This concept is widely applicable in business settings. It is often applied in the form of a Pareto chart—a special type of histogram (bar graph) used to graphically display causes of a problem in order of severity from largest to smallest. Remedial action can be focused on the areas that will yield the greatest results. This is widely used in Six Sigma programs.

Then rank those same customers in descending annual profit contribution. Use the available information such as annual budgets for gross-margin dollars, to get started. More refined measures of profit are also useful later on.

Next, rank those same customers in descending order of percentage gross margin. Lay all three lists side by side. The names at the top of the first two lists should be similar. The percentage list may have a very different assortment of customers at the top.

Next, go to the top and bottom of the sales and margin lists and find the 20 percent cumulative and 80 percent cumulative points and draw lines across the list. You have now identified the most valuable and least valuable customers from a sales and profit contribution perspective. Among those lowest volume and least profitable customers is where complexity usually hides.

Carefully analyze the list of margin percentages and compare it to the list of margin dollars. A very high margin percentage with a customer that contributes little in sales and little in profits is usually an indication of a customer that may add unnecessary complexity. Remember, none of the cost systems track complexity costs, so they must be identified through other means.

Do the descending-order ranking on suppliers and annual purchase dollars too. Complexity exists both on the sell side and the buy side. Draw the 20 percent and 80 percent lines on that listing too. Just as you looked for the obvious customers that added more complexity than sales or profits, look for the suppliers who fall into that same category. Examine these carefully for the likely causes of complexity.

Finally, repeat this ranking process for finished products by annual sales volume and gross-margin dollar and gross-margin percentage contributions listed in descending order. Draw the 80 percent/20 percent lines and you will see the same issues there. A common excuse for keeping products that add complexity but not profit is "we need them to fill out the line." That is usually nothing more than an excuse. And where it is true, analyze the "line" it fills out and the customers who buy that line to assure that the overall line is handsomely profitable.

In any turnaround situation, these descending lists are the first things a turnaround specialist will ask for and analyze. It is ideal to review them at least quarterly and perhaps monthly to see where a company is making money and where it is not. If there are high-margin products where a sizable volume increase is possible, these are opportunities upon which to focus attention. Few actions improve profitability more than shifting the sales mix to higher profit-margin products (or customers). Once this data and these analyses become a systemic part of the company's management processes, complexity will have a much tougher time hiding.

Calculate Sales and Margin per SKU

One of the simplest and most common metrics to measure return versus complexity is to calculate the sales (revenue) and profit margin per "stock-keeping unit" (SKU). In most cases, the approach to metrics will be described from the perspective of a product-based company.

Most of the internally driven causes of complexity arise first from products, but services are products, too, and can be counted and categorized in almost the same way. Each time a specific service is added to those offered, the risk of adding complexity exists just as it does with products.

Next, most of the externally driven complexity arises from the wrong mix of customers—or from responses to competitors' actions.

Customers are defined as the entity that pays you for whatever you sell. In a consumer-products instance, it might be a retailer or a consumer. In a utility, it is the user of electricity, gas, water, etc. In a leisure setting it is a guest at the theme park, restaurant, or hotel. For financial-services providers it is the investor, the bank depositor, or borrower, etc. Customers can be counted and so can suppliers. Locations/facilities can also be readily counted, irrespective of their nature. Legal entities are easily counted, regardless of whether it is a product or service sold. The problem is that many companies never actually "count" these sources of complexity.

Using the sales and margin per SKU provides a way to identify how much revenue and gross margin is generated by each individual item you sell. This is important because it costs money to create and maintain each item. Another useful way to look at this information is in a few more of those descending-order lists, this time ranked by annual revenue per SKU and annual margin contribution per SKU. The best, highest-revenue and highest-margin contribution products will be at the top, and the bottom will be filled with mostly losers—the by-products of unrealized complexity.

Hopefully, the same items will populate the top of both lists, but this is not necessarily what happens. There are often products that contribute high sales revenue but not correspondingly high profit-margin contributions. This can be an issue if too much of your capacity is directed at less-profitable products, and not coincidentally, less-profitable customers.

If the Complexity Crisis has seriously impacted the business, even the 80–20 rule will start to shift to a 70/30 or 60/40, indicating that the revenues and profits are not as concentrated, and perhaps that overproliferation has diluted this normal situation. Some businesses are actually different and the 80–20 rule doesn't apply, but before using the "we're different" excuse, look hard for evidence of complexity at work.

Analyze Sales per Customer (or Market)

A few years ago, Larry Selden and Geoffrey Colvin came out with a book germane to the whole issue of complexity, entitled *Angel Customers and Demon Customers*. The essential message of the book is clear. Too often we simply look at products/product lines to investigate overall profitability. We too seldom look at our customers' overall profitability. According to the authors' findings, the 80–20 rule applies here, too, but a little differently. It seems that about 20 percent of the customers actually were so profitable that they created most of the value for the shareholders of the company. Another 20 percent were so unprofitable that they destroyed shareholder value. And 60 percent fell in the middle somewhere, waiting to be moved up—or out. This meant that after a bout with the Complexity Crisis, there was a very good chance that the bottom 20 percent group may have grown, usually at the expense of the top 20 percent. This is bad for profitability. A more sophisticated model can consider cost to serve and program costs to arrive at more accurate overall customer profitability numbers and enhance this analysis.

Just as ranking sales per product in descending dollar order exposes unproductive and money-losing products, a list of sales per customer will expose many complexity-related customer issues. When companies proliferate customers to increase sales, these new customers often show up at the bottom of such rankings. At the bottom of these lists, you are certain to find customers who need to be "fired," or at least turned over to distributors who can serve them economically, albeit with the customers paying correspondingly higher prices. The customers and products that occupy the bottom of these lists are those that add complexity without the redeeming feature of adding profitability. Get rid of them.

Occasionally some truly high-potential customers will show up with low sales when they are new to a company. These are usually well-known prospects and deserve to be nurtured and cultivated while they grow and move up the ranking. The most common defense for many small, marginal customers is "that customer buys a really profitable assortment." This is usually nonsense, since the cost of handling small orders with a high variety of items is extremely high and eats up all of the (high-margin) profit and then some.

Sales per Employee

The last of the more common metrics, but still only used sparingly, is to compute sales (revenue) per employee and profit per employee. This may need to be done on a business-unit basis, possibly on a plant or division basis to get enough of the local market influence in the calculation. There's plenty of available benchmarking information on sales per employee for various types of industries, processes, plants, etc.

These are not fine-tune measures; they are sort of like the doctor taking a temperature, blood pressure, and so on. If the reading is okay, the patient (and the company) might be okay. If it is not, something is probably wrong and there's a need to investigate further. In situations where complexity has infected a company, such measures will not be okay. Complexity requires added staff to manage and this shows in higher headcount without a correspondingly higher level of sales.

If the data from these types of measures are compiled into a trailing twelve-month graphical format, trends will become apparent—good or bad. Watch the direction of the line carefully. A noticeable rise is likely an indicator of the impact of complexity.

The Complexity Factor (CF)

Now that we have dealt with a couple of the routine physical-exam-type metrics, let's move to a new metric that is more complex to compile but also quite revealing in its relative simplicity. Let's call it the Complexity Factor (CF).

A Benchmarking Tool

One of the problems in diagnosing and treating complexity is the fact that there are no established metrics to use. I previously cited some common metrics that will help, but each was isolated to a particular part of the problem—one for products, one for customers, and so forth. It is time to address the fact that no overall metrics currently exist to track or warn of this complexity phenomenon—until now.

A simple calculation (a single number for the CF) can be a sufficient signal that something is wrong here. It is analogous to a doctor noting a person's elevated temperature to indicate the presence of an illness. Unlike the pulse or blood pressure, which can be temporarily elevated for superficial reasons, the body temperature is a more significant and meaningful measurement. When it starts rising, it signals that something in the body is amiss, and that something warrants attention and possible treatment. Also like the body-temperature measurement, the CF is not a definitive metric for detailed diagnoses, but it can be a very useful tool whose strong message is "look further." Arguably, one of the greatest values of the CF is as a self-benchmarking tool to watch rise or fall as changes are made that add or remove complexity.

A Progress Measurement

All organizations need metrics that tell them whether they are making progress or not, and at how rapid a rate that progress is occurring. This positive (or negative) reinforcement helps leaders keep the organization on track and motivated to move forward with even more vigor. Broad progress measures also need to be easy to understand and calculate, so the larger part of the organization can understand how and how much their efforts "move the needle." When measures are complex or difficult to understand, rationalizations and excuses pop up about why more progress is not being made. The CF has no such mystique. Few parts of it are even subject to "interpretation."

A Simple Calculation

Calculating a CF is simple—*if* companies have the information readily available (most don't, even though they should and easily can have the information). In fact, not having the necessary information at hand is no reason to hesitate. It is possible to use today's sophisticated information technology to gather most of the necessary information fairly rapidly.

Here's how to do it. This example will use a "product" business, but a service business can substitute its own definition of "products" and make a similar calculation. While the CF alone doesn't work as well in comparing widely differing businesses (e.g., product businesses to service businesses) it is still directionally useful. One thing is sure: When the CF goes up, profitability nearly always goes down.

CALCULATING THE COMPLEXITY FACTOR

(CF) = Number of Finished Products (SKUs) ×
Number of Different Markets Served ×
Number of Company Legal Entities ×
Number of (Significant) Facilities ×
(Number of Employees + Number of Suppliers + Number of Customers) ÷
by Sales Revenues

Let's take an example of three hypothetical competing product companies with their relative Complexity Factors and two other conventional metrics, sales per SKU and sales per employee, that are indicative of different complexity-related symptoms.

Three Different Product Companies

Company A does $135,000,000 in sales; it has 1,200 SKUs, and sells them into just 2 different markets—a mass retail market and a specialty shop market, but does so in 4 different countries where legal entities exist, using 3 facilities. It has only 50 employees (it has outsourced nearly everything), 70 suppliers (highly concentrated), but 3,900 customers due to the nature of its chosen distribution. Let's do the calculation for the Complexity Factor, as instructed in the previous box:

$1,200 \times 2 \times 4 \times 3 \times (50 + 70 + 3900) \div 135,000,000 = $ CF of 0.35
Sales per SKU = $112,500
Sales per Customer = $90,000
Sales per Employee = $2,700,000

Initial research has shown that companies with a CF of less than 1.0 have managed to avoid the most common problems of complexity. This company has a good chance of being quite profitable, assuming its products are well designed and positioned versus the competition in its markets. It could be even more profitable if it were to rationalize its customer base, and reduce the number of customers served.

Company B does $540,000,000 in sales; it has 5,000 SKUs and sells them into 15 different markets and does so in 6 different countries/continents where legal entities exist, using 10 facilities. It has 3,000 employees, 2,500 suppliers, and 2,300 customers. Its calculation is:

$$5,000 \times 15 \times 6 \times 10 \times (3,000 + 2,500 + 2,300) \div 540,000,000 = \text{CF of } 65$$
Sales per SKU = $ 108,000
Sales per Customer = $235,000
Sales per Employee = $180,000

Preliminary research has also shown that companies with a CF of over 50 are unnecessarily complex and offer large opportunities for improvement. This company is fairly complex and, thus, it is likely not as profitable as it might be. It has opportunities in several areas (SKUs, suppliers, customers) to reduce complexity, which should improve profitability.

Company C does $1.8 billion in sales; it has 3,000 SKUs and sells them into only 2 primary markets, but does so in 15 different countries where legal entities exist, using 25 facilities. It has 4,000 employees, 7,000 suppliers, and 2,000 customers:

$$3000 \times 2 \times 15 \times 25 \times (4{,}000 + 7{,}000 + 2{,}000) \div 1{,}600{,}000{,}000 = CF \text{ of } 16$$

Sales per SKU = $600,000
Sales per Customer = $900,000
Sales per Employee = $450,000

When companies fall into the CF range of 1 through 50, a deeper understanding of their causes of complexity is required. These may be companies that are struggling with a decision to either drive out complexity or to capitalize on it. This is a midrange company in its complexity, and it could be reasonably profitable. Clearly the high sales volume helps reduce the CF in spite of a relatively large number of suppliers, which represents a large area for improvement, but because of its large geographic base of sales—fifteen countries—reducing this number of suppliers may be difficult.

As stated earlier, the Complexity Factor is not an absolute measure—it is an indicator, like a thermometer, that provides information about the likelihood of a company suffering from complexity or benefiting from the lack of it. As more and more companies learn to compute and track their CFs, more data will become available. Along with this data will be a better granularity regarding the consequences of the amount and nature of the complexity, and its relative impact on profitability. Since this is a whole new field of measurement, progress is likely to be rapid and dramatic. The more traditional metrics of sales per employee, per SKU, and per customer provide additional information, some of which can be easily benchmarked against other similar industry competitors.

What any metric such as the Complexity Factor ignores in its quantitative nature are the qualitative issues such as the company's structure and process configurations and the competitive/marketing strategy. In Chapter 16, we will see that there are times when complexity can be used for strategic competitive advantage, but the company using it must understand the nature of the game it is playing, and structure itself accordingly. At other times, eliminating the complexity and reaping benefits of lower costs and greater speed might be a far more powerful strategic approach. Use the CF as a key benchmark for your business. Calculate it regularly (at least monthly), and plot it on a trailing twelve-month graph and then drive it down—or understand why it went up—and make sure that added complexity is really paying off based on the competitive strategies being employed.

TAC #6: COMPLEXITY IS THE ENEMY

Drive down the CF; drive up the profitability of the company.

New Accounting Standards—A Professional Opportunity

The development of the Complexity Factor offers a great opportunity for the accounting profession, its regulatory bodies, and its leading firms to adopt an important new metric. Accounting has long used indices such as this to monitor performance and progress in its review of companies' performance and controls. If the General Accounting Standards Board and the five to ten largest public accounting firms would adopt the Complexity Factor computation as a standard accounting metric, a database could be created within industry types. For the first time ever, the drivers of hidden costs of complexity could no longer remain hidden. Companies would also have new benchmarking information against which to measure progress.

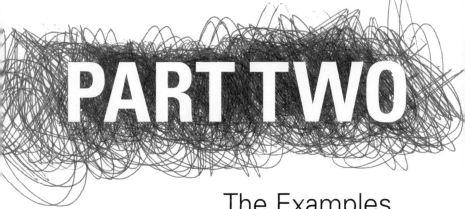

The Examples

SUBS AND SUNDAES

Subway and Dairy Queen Compete by Managing Complexity

"Simplicity does not precede complexity, but follows it."
—Alan J. Perlis

Subway sandwich shops are everywhere one looks in the United States. In these small, make-to-order, deli-style restaurants, Subway uses a limited number of basic ingredients and can produce a nearly infinite variety of sandwiches. Most readers have probably seen the Subway process of build to order. Fresh-baked bread, in perhaps a half-dozen varieties (it used to be just three), four kinds of meat, three kinds of cheese, an array of vegetables—perhaps twenty of them—and condiments—six dressings. When you order, you select ingredients and the sandwich builder adds your choices to the desired size of sandwich and on the style of bread you chose. The bread is the platform—choose a 6-inch or 12-inch (they cut the 12-inch loaf in half for a 6-inch sandwich and use the remainder for a future order). Or, now you can also get a popular wrap variation—but just in one size.

One of the benefits of competing with complexity is that, like the Dell Computer model, minor variations can be added easily because the structure and process are designed to be less sensitive to that kind of complexity. Want a warm sandwich? Subway can just pop it into the warmer, which is situated behind the counter. Want a salad? Eliminate the bread and load up on vegetables and, if you wish, sliced cheese and meat. Chips are available in one of four or five flavors—and you pull the bag off the rack and place it on the counter to pay for it. And (my favorite), finally, fresh-baked chocolate-chip cookies (that I'm sure are high-margin items). Oh, yes, for drinks—one size fits all there, too, and you dispense your own, leaving the sandwich builder(s) free to assemble sandwiches for other customers, and/or collect at the register.

This model uses all of the solutions discussed previously for competing with complexity. Postponement is a big one, waiting until the very last moment before customizing the product to the customer's wishes. So is mass customization. Bread is baked slightly ahead of the mealtime rushes, using idle time of the sandwich maker productively, and baking multiple loaves of each kind at one time. The meats, cheeses, vegetables, and condiments trays are stocked in idle time, too, but from mass-processed foods, delivered to the restaurants in sealed bags.

This is a perfectly simple and familiar example of the principles of adapting the structure and processes to the "use it" strategy of competing on intentionally created complexity. Once the store managers know how much of each main ingredient is consumed in a given time period, it can be reordered, supplied, or prepared during idle time between meal-time rushes. Inventory obsolescence is minimal, limited to the bread that is left over due to the wrong mix sold compared to what was baked. Complexity that is driven by consumer choice at the time of demand is a competitive advantage.

Dairy Queen and Baskin-Robbins Grew Using Complexity

Frozen custard-style ice cream became a widely sold dessert item decades ago, long before concepts like competing on complexity, postponement, or mass customization had even been invented. The Dairy Queen franchise was built around the custard-dispensing machine, which took the liquid custard and froze it into a semisolid and then dispensed it through a nozzle into cones, sundae dishes, or milkshake cups. The accompanying items were cones in two styles—cake and sugar; nuts, whipped cream, a large array of flavoring fruit/syrup (chocolate, hot fudge, caramel, strawberry, marshmallow, etc.), and later, mix-in items such as crushed Oreo cookies, crumbled Heath candy bars, M&Ms, and waffle cones were added. From this small array of sweets and the platform of the frozen-custard machine, a wide variety of confections could be created.

Cones, sundaes, and milkshakes were the staples until competition matched that assortment, upon which DQ introduced the "Blizzard," the "Shiver," and other creative combinations of the same ingredients using an adaptation of the milkshake mixer to make more and more different delectables for kids and adults alike. A trip to the Dairy Queen wasn't a culinary event; it was a family outing and a sort of ceremony of celebration to reward good grades or other family good fortune.

Who Needs 31 Flavors of Ice Cream?

After the DQ success, a company entered the ice cream market with a new approach. Baskin-Robbins's 31 flavors of ice cream introduced purposeful complexity. Who needs 31 flavors of ice cream? No one does. But this approach drew people, who were seeking new and different ice cream flavor experiences. Baskin-Robbins also charged handsomely for its high variety, with premium prices as much as twice the normal price for ice cream cones. People came and bought. The stores were successful and have survived to this day. One of Baskin-Robbins's marketing tools was to reinforce the quality of the ice cream with small signs on the walls containing sayings, such as this: "There is scarcely anything in the world that some man cannot make a little worse, and sell a little more cheaply. The person who buys on price alone is this man's lawful prey." (That one is by John Ruskin, writer, art critic, and philosopher.)

Although frozen yogurt stores like TCBY and regional ice cream chains have taken market share from DQ, its original principle of competing on complexity remains virtually unchanged. To compete with the Baskin-Robbins stores, premium ice cream stores have now started using a technique of mixing up custom ice cream flavors on a marble slab. Three or four plain ice cream flavors are used as the platform and a wide range of ingredients are folded into the ice cream on a make-to-order basis—and for a premium price, of course. Competing using complexity works well *if* the structure and processes are designed for it.

Plan Global, Make Local

Whatever the method and the product, it is clear that some situations are ripe for competing on complexity, whether the product is a computer or a confection. The principle of "thinking global but acting local" is also at work here. The choices that are most popular may vary by state, city, or even neighborhood. That makes no difference since the system accommodates variety and easy adjustment to local conditions based on a global platform, structure, and processes.

When customers choose a Subway sandwich or a Dairy Queen dessert—or a Dell Computer—the ingredients are combined into the specific one the customer wants, and this is all done at the last possible minute. This form of competing-on-complexity system can also take advantage of the laws of compensating errors in forecasting and planning. It matters little which kinds of meat, cheese, vegetables, or condiments are chosen, as long as the same platforms—breads—are used. This means a simple last-minute selection is all that manages the mix change. As more of one item is consumed and less of another, the store manager simply adjusts future ordering to bring inventory back in line. Some might contend that such an approach isn't that easy in business, but if the product design and systems architecture are done properly, complexity can be a differentiator for your business—without crippling it.

CARS

How Many Models Is Just Enough?

> "Leadership is the courage to admit mistakes, the vision to welcome change, the enthusiasm to motivate others, and the confidence to stay out of step when everyone else is marching to the wrong tune."
> —E. M. Estes, former Chairman and CEO, General Motors

Ford Versus GM—a History Lesson

America has long had a love affair with the automobile. Daimler and Benz may have invented the first cars in Germany, but few people have had a greater influence on the development of the automobile and the global auto industry than Henry Ford and Alfred Sloan (of General Motors). There are few places in the history of industrial development where one could find a better example of complexity's impact than the past century in the U.S. auto industry. Complexity evolved, became a competitive advantage, reversed itself, and is now beginning to rise again.

Ford's Model T: Ultimate Simplicity—One Model

Henry Ford invented the equivalent of the modern-day assembly line. In doing so, he realized that its best productive use was to make just one model—the Model T—in one color—black. Make no mistake, Ford was still a complex company because it made a strategic decision to be vertically integrated. Vertical integration is when you make almost everything you need for yourself instead of buying it from outside suppliers; for example, Ford owned iron ore mines, smelters, and steel mills. Given that the auto industry was still in its infancy—and thus didn't have much support infrastructure—this ownership provided Ford with the supplies he needed. In one sense, it added immense complexity, but in another, it reduced complexity by reducing the number of external suppliers Ford had to use. For example, when it came to steel, Ford had to deal with only one supplier—its own captive steel mill.

Henry Ford then made two essential decisions. The first was to abandon the common industry practice of producing many different models, and instead make just one model, and to make it in just one color. This simplified so many things: It eliminated the need to changeover components, paint colors, accessories, and everything else, and it made the assembly line much more productive. Ford concentrated on breaking up the assembly line jobs into small pieces of work, making each job far less complex and permitting the workers to learn their individual job much more rapidly. Productivity soared and the cost of a Model T allowed more Americans than ever to afford an automobile.

The first Model T was a good value at $825 for a 1,200-pound car with a twenty-horsepower engine and a two-speed, foot-controlled planetary transmission. It was sturdy, reliable, and versatile. But Ford wasn't done yet. He stated his goal: "I'm going to democratize the automobile. When I'm through, everybody will be able to afford one and everybody will have one."

With this aim in mind, Ford further cut prices as he added that era's version of automation and assembly line job design. From $220 in 1909, Ford cut the price to $99 in 1914 and sales exploded to a quarter of a million cars—almost half of the U.S. auto market. Ford proved three things. First, a strategic, systematic lowering of prices could boost volume and increase profits. Second, the elimination of complexity had a wonderful effect on efficiency and productivity. At Ford, in 1913, 13,000 workers made 260,000 cars, whereas the rest of the industry required 66,000 workers to make just 10 percent more, or 286,000 cars. Third, the elimination of complexity in jobs allowed workers to remain stationary and perform repetitive tasks faster and faster, as the chain-driven assembly line speeded up the production pace. While this approach had considerable downsides (monotony, fatigue, boredom, etc.), it made cars fast and cheaply.

Alfred Sloan and GM—a Different Way

In the early 1920s, GM was a conglomeration of car companies and parts suppliers, but Alfred Sloan had already begun to chip away at Ford's dominant market position. A better transmission was one piece of the attack. Improved, updated styling was another. As Ford's prices steadily rose to $290 in the mid-1920s, styling and excitement over a new car grew, as did GM's market position. Alfred Sloan articulated GM's product strategy of creating "a car for every purse and purpose" in his "Message to Shareholders" in the company's 1924 Annual Report. Sloan's strategy was to use the purposeful addition of complexity as a competitive weapon against Ford's concentration on a single model.

But Sloan didn't stop there. Once he had Ford on the run, Sloan continued to innovate in ways that used complexity to competitive advantage. Ford finally introduced the Model A and a few different colors in 1928 and 1929, but by then its market position had begun to deteriorate due to GM's attacks. Sloan wisely decided to create a reason for people to replace their cars before they wore out. It was called the annual model changeover. This added considerable complexity in parts, production, dealer inventories, and more, but it also shot GM to the top of the U.S. auto industry.

Sloan's "car for every purse and purpose" allowed him to segment the market by socioeconomic status and offer cars ranging from entry-level Chevrolets (for the working family) to Pontiac (a sportier Chevy), Oldsmobile (near luxury), Buick (the doctor's car), and Cadillac (a car for the rich). This segmentation strategy was both brilliant and successful. It could even withstand a change from the unduly complex (but highly desirable planned obsolescence) of the annual model changeover, to model changes that spanned a few years. What finally killed this strategy and began GM's long slide into its current tenuous state were the mistakes of GM chairman Roger Smith's era in the 1980s.

Smith's staff urged him to rethink the sheer number of brands and models, and with the best of intentions, GM created common car platforms. That was not a bad idea in itself, which Chrysler later proved. Platform designs can help contain complexity while providing easier brand/customer differentiation.

GM had paid far too much to its union employees during the period from the 1930s to the 1970s, and thus its cost structure was strained. As Smith's GM tried to make differentiated cars using common platforms, it failed miserably in the execution and missed a major strategic point. The cars all looked too much alike, and the brand/model differentiation was transparently superficial. Sloan's car for every purse and purpose meant that Chevrolet buyers neither wanted nor could afford "luxurious" Chevrolets, and Cadillac buyers certainly didn't want "cheaper" Chevrolets dressed in Cadillac emblems and unnecessary chrome trim. The problem was in the execution and use of those platforms. GM's car divisions were like warring tribes, fighting for resources, while refusing to cooperate or collaborate.

Complexity caused by model-year changeovers was a nonissue when the other two large U.S. auto companies had adopted the same strategy. The complexity added by the "car for every purse and purpose" strategy had also been largely emulated by Ford and Chrysler as both created additional brands (Mercury and Lincoln for Ford and Plymouth, Desoto, and Dodge for Chrysler). With the U.S. market encapsulated in a way that all competitors were employing similar strategies from a complexity standpoint, there was no meaningful complexity-based advantage or disadvantage.

When Mercedes-Benz entered the U.S. super-luxury market in the late 1950s, Cadillac could have competed with the company if it chose to (creating a competitive premium model), and slowed or stopped the invasion. When the Japanese entered the low-end, small-car market, U.S. makers likewise abdicated the low end of the market instead of making good, small, fuel-efficient cars to compete, even if they had to sell them at little or at no profit to protect that segment of the market.

But neither of those things happened, and thanks to those strategic missteps, the U.S. auto industry set the stage for the Japanese to use the "lose it" version of a complexity-based strategy and capture a strong foothold in the U.S. auto market. Meanwhile, European (and later Japanese) luxury carmakers took direct aim at GM's Cadillac and Ford's Lincoln markets, with great success.

GM—Too Many Brands, Too Much Complexity

Today, GM still suffers from complexity that it cannot seem to eliminate fast enough. Cutting the Oldsmobile brand was a painful but necessary step. Now GM only has about twice as many auto brands as its market share can support. Chevrolet, Buick, and Cadillac are keepers with fairly clear brand images and strong competitive positions. Now consider the following GM brands: Saab, Saturn, GMC, Hummer, and Pontiac. Eight brands is too many, adding huge doses of complexity in both product/production and dealer/distribution—not to mention all the duplication/fragmentation in divisional staffing, design, and advertising. In addition to its core brands, GM still has remnants of involvement with some lesser Japanese brands and even a joint venture with Toyota (the Fremont, California, plant).

Sloan's original choice of five brands might be about right for GM in the twenty-first century. The challenge is how to get there *fast*. It won't be easy, but if GM is to survive and compete, it must make further Draconian cuts—starting with brands and plant capacity and ending with outdated and unaffordable legacy costs.

The Japanese Defeat Complexity—the Transition to Foreign Auto Dominance

Japan's defeat in World War II allowed it to rebuild its industrial infrastructure anew, starting from a current knowledge and competitive base. From the teachings of American quality gurus J. M. Juran and W. Edwards Deming, the Japanese realized that complexity undermines quality, which led to Japan's quality strategy. Understanding how complexity adds unnecessary cost led to the product strategy that Japan would use to build what has now become a dominant U.S. market position—in mind share if not yet in actual share.

American Carmakers' Strategy: Variety, Change, and Complexity

During their glory days, the allure of U.S. carmakers resided in their customers' ability to custom-order cars with a long list of options, and then wait for those cars to be built and delivered. Dealers stocked a few models with the most popular options, but these were mostly for show and test drives. Mathematics shows that the combinations and permutations of dozens or hundreds of options, colors, and body styles can lead to millions of possible models. Thus, the standardization of the assembly line that worked so well for Henry Ford was gone entirely.

American carmakers' assembly lines in the 1950–1970 era were "customized build" lines, and between high-cost labor and complexity of a near infinite variety, and noncooperation of GM divisions, such lines were anything but efficient. Further, the huge variety of parts, options, and models combined with the frequent design changes made build quality mediocre at best, terrible at worst. Details that were built incorrectly were left to the delivering dealer to fix, often after delivering the car to the excited buyer—only to find that the windows leaked, trim fell off, pieces didn't fit properly, and worse.

Japan's Strategy: Quality and Simplicity

As post–WWII Japan rebuilt itself, U.S. quality experts Juran and Deming taught it the importance of reducing variability to achieve high quality. Japan also learned about robust designs, in which considering how a product would be fabricated and assembled could eliminate quality problems. Most of all, Japanese carmakers realized that offering only a few variations—perhaps four exterior colors and two interior colors—and equipping all cars with the most popular options made it easier and more economical to build cars, which led to higher build quality. This is the essence of eliminating the Complexity Factor—the "lose it" version.

Suddenly, it seemed, the association of Japan and poorly made products was transformed as small, fuel-efficient, reliable Japanese cars began arriving in the United States—just as the 1970s oil-shock drove gas prices up and limited supply. While the skyrocketing oil prices couldn't have been planned strategically, it did give the Japanese carmakers just the break they needed. The large, gas-guzzling V-8 engines in U.S. cars now consumed more fuel, and more-expensive high-octane fuel. The most desirable options on U.S. cars increased their price, plus customers had to order them and then wait six to eight weeks (or more) for them to be built.

Japanese cars arrived with the most popular features—AM/FM/cassette-tape systems, power features, air conditioning, and more—as standard features. The few colors selected, while not exciting, were neutral enough to be acceptable to the large middle market—black, white, silver, etc. Here were reliable, economical cars, with all the best features ready to roll right off the dealers' lots, and at attractive prices. The U.S. auto industry would never recover. Japanese cars didn't have annual model changeovers, so the styles didn't appear to be obsolete in a year or two. They also didn't break down often; parts fit; accessories worked; and U.S. consumers bought them. As time went on, the Japanese hired California design studios to improve styling to match U.S. tastes.

The Japanese cars grew in size, but the basic principles remained—use fewer colors and include popular options either as standard features or grouped in fewer packages. As Chapter Four discusses, Japanese suppliers were fewer in number and located close to automakers' plants, thus variability and in-process inventory were both reduced. These factors, combined with the more robust designs (learned in part from the involvement with quality gurus Juran and Deming), resulted in the build quality of the cars being much better than that of U.S.-made cars.

To this day, decades after the first Honda arrived in the United States, it has only two brands—Honda and Acura (a luxury brand). Toyota, until recently adding Scion, had only two—Toyota and Lexus. The same applied for Nissan (Nissan and Infiniti).

One of the most striking contrasts was in the legacy GM had of divisional autonomy versus the Japanese ability to start "clean." At one time, GM had 20 different fuel pumps and 26 different seat frames. Toyota, for example, has 2 different seat frames. GM made about a dozen different engines, while the Japanese carmakers have a few each, but the number is closer to half the GM complexity. GM is making progress—the fuel pumps are down from 20 to 6—but there is a huge complexity gap to close. The Japanese learned well the lessons of how unmanaged complexity creates hidden costs, worse quality, and inferior service—and avoided it from the outset. Only now is Toyota considering slowing its rate of global new-model intro-duction because of concerns about initial quality. It has grown to number two in the United States and is a large global producer, thus it must keep growing complexity on its radar screen, lest it repeat others' mistakes.

Focus Drives Out Complexity

The lessons from the auto industry are so numerous and so obvi-ous that further explanation seems unnecessary. It clearly illustrates the way Alfred Sloan's GM chose to "use it" and make proliferation and purposeful complexity into a competitive advantage. That com-petitive advantage held up as long as competitors were playing the same game. As the Japanese began to focus on making fewer, better, and more well-equipped models, and changing the styles less often, it upset the competitive apple cart.

When Japanese carmakers Honda and Toyota started playing the "lose it" game, wringing out complexity, simplifying models and variations down to a few, and then making each of them superbly, Sloan's "use it" complexity-based strategy showed its vulnerability. The leadership insularity and inward focus of GM further delayed its understanding of how badly it was being beaten, which postponed any meaningful corrective action for years. The fact that the other American automakers had all followed Sloan's complexity-based strategy made them all vulnerable to this type of competitive attack.

Mistakes at GM—and Cadillac

When the American car companies tried to react to the Japanese strategy, they lost focus on what each of their cars meant to their consumers, and even more embarrassing mistakes followed. GM's luxury brand, Cadillac, made some of the most egregious errors; mistakes which cost them market share, prestige, and sales for several decades. Consider just a couple of these errors.

During the 1980s as GM attempted to drive out complexity in its own misguided way, it created a series of platform vehicles for its Buick, Oldsmobile, and Pontiac divisions that were almost indistinguishable from one another—at least in the eyes of its customers. Not only did GM simplify things poorly, it left an underlying complexity of its "warring faction" divisional and a huge dealer network in place, to pretend that these look-alike, work-alike vehicles were actually different. They weren't—and consumers knew it.

Another of the overused, yet instructional examples of GM's misadventures was with its Cadillac brand and how it confused brand identities in its product/brand mix. Is a Chevy a small, economical car, and a Cadillac a large, comfortable car? Sure they are. Then a Chevrolet Cavalier dressed up and re-badged as a Cadillac was still a small car that looked a lot like a much cheaper Chevy Cavalier. Then there was the more recent one—the Catera. But what is a Catera? "A Caddy that zigs" was the advertising positioning. It was a small Cadillac that looked more like a Chevy. It wasn't a bad car, based on a good Opel platform (GM's European model). It was just a bad brand-positioning mistake. Most Cadillac buyers didn't want a small "Caddy that zigs," they want a big, luxurious, and comfortable status symbol—which was what Cadillac had been for years.

Finally, the largest Chevrolet—the Impala—grew to behemoth size, as large as the pricier Cadillacs. This totally confused the two brand's identities (big cars, little cars, cheap cars, expensive cars, etc.). In GM's desperate search of growth and cost savings simultaneously, more complexity was created and it confused consumers, casting doubt on both products, and damaging at least one brand (the more highly regarded one—Cadillac). These are errors that GM finally seems to have figured out, but only after two decades of missteps.

PLANES AND COMPUTERS

Examples of Complexity Controlled—
and Gone Wild

"Everything should be made as simple as possible, but not simpler."
—Albert Einstein

The airline industry is a business drowning in complexity. For starters, there is a mind-boggling array of fare structures for any given flight. Try making arrangements far in advance and you may get a great price. Or wait until just a couple of weeks before your intended travel date in hopes of getting a last-minute deal . . . if there is anything available. Once you actually make a reservation, don't try to change it, or you'll pay a penalty (which can approximate the cost of a ticket) and your fare will change to the fare "then in effect" (usually higher). God forbid that you cancel your travel plans and end up with an unused ticket. If you try to apply that $250 unused ticket, you will be assessed a $100 to $130 change fee and a fare difference of $115. (In the example I checked, the fare had risen from $250 to $365.) When finished, using that $250 ticket will end up costing you an additional $245. Of course, there were twenty other flights available with many other, different fare structures, but those would have cost even more and been less convenient. What a complex mess.

Airlines defend pricing complexity by basing it on "yield management" pricing theory (price vs. supply vs. demand vs. time). They vary prices based on the time remaining before the actual flight date and how full the flight is at that time. Airlines also adjust prices up and down to different customers and for different times, even for different parts of the airplane. In their zeal to charge as much as possible yet fill the plane as full as possible, most airlines don't have any (quantifiable) idea how much this complexity costs in lost productivity, systems complexity, confusion, and customer ill will.

Fares, discounts, advance-booking prices, and so forth are only one part of the airlines' complexity problem. Air travel is an inherently complex business in the first place, and this is complicated by the fact that it is weather dependent. The hub-and-spoke system used by most major airlines seems ideal to distribute travelers to a wide variety of places, but it has other inherent problems—like the ripple effect. When weather is bad in Chicago or Atlanta (the two busiest U.S. airports), flight delays on connections through those two hubs can cause delays to ripple throughout the United States, and often internationally, too. A midafternoon thunderstorm at O'Hare in Chicago might only delay flights for 30 to 45 minutes, but with a plane landing every minute, that's 30 to 40 planes that will be delayed. And if that storm lasts over an hour, there will be missed connections requiring rerouting, lines at ticket counters, and unplanned overnight stays. Just replanning the entire schedule of flights, aircraft, crews, and seating is a complex job.

Probably nowhere in the cost systems of airline companies is there an accounting "factor" that calculates how complexity adds cost, as differences on fares, routes, and disruptions like mechanical failures, airport traffic delays, and weather problems are piled onto complex schedules for thousands of passengers on hundreds of flights on any given day. The marketing departments of airlines add to the complexity—with the best of intentions—by devising new promotions to drive traffic into particular markets, each of which gets layered atop all of the others.

A few airlines, most notably Southwest, seem to have "broken the code" by simplifying how it operates to thwart the worst effects of complexity. First, it has fewer different fares. Second, it flies fewer kinds of planes (one), which leads to simpler maintenance management. It offers one seating plan—first checked in, first seated. It offers one meal plan—none. And, it turns its planes around in less time, thus flying (and generating revenue) more of the time than competitors.

Major airlines are finally learning from Southwest. Just a few years ago, major airlines led by United, American, Delta, and to a lesser extent, USAir, Northwest, and Continental, had too many different types of planes and different seating configurations within plane type. At one time, a few years ago, American was reported to have seventeen different kinds of aircraft in service and multiple seating configurations within that variety of planes. Substituting equipment to compensate for mechanical problems or weather delays often meant reconfiguring the seat assignments (at best) or even bumping confirmed passengers off flights (at worst) because the replacement aircraft didn't have as many seats. There was also a need for "downgrades" where passengers booked in first class had to move to coach because of fewer seats available in first class.

Interchangeability of planes for Southwest is easy. For the others, interchanging planes was more difficult for both fliers and airline employees alike. Southwest flies largely point to point, with only a few connections, thus minimizing the places where it could get caught in those ripple delays. New, low-fare airlines and connector lines using smaller commuter jets are starting to emulate this practice, yielding lower fares and better on-time service, bypassing congested hubs.

What Southwest must avoid is the mistakes that killed the first "simple airline," People's Express, a couple of decades ago—adding complexity to an inherently simple business model. It went from simple to complex in its efforts to compete in too many markets. Complexity ended up being the fatal blow at People's Express, and one that could threaten the new upstart, Jet Blue, due to complexity created by its rapid growth.

What Ryanair Learned as Southwest Airlines Beat American

Others are now emulating Southwest's complexity-free model. Ireland's Ryanair was just another struggling airline operating in Europe instead of the United States. In 1991, Michael O'Leary, Ryanair's chief executive, visited Dallas to meet with Southwest's executives. He took back the lessons he learned and completely rethought how Ryanair would operate. Like Southwest, he focused on one kind of airplane, the venerable Boeing 737, and chose to serve smaller, secondary airports. Ryanair also emulated Southwest's open seating plan, which reduces work for airport staff and speeds the boarding process.

Since then, Ryanair has gone further, striving to drive down costs in every aspect of its operation. O'Leary states, "We want to be known as the Wal-Mart of flying." One might question if he is going too far when Ryanair eliminated free checked baggage, charging $3.50 per piece and charging for all refreshments on flights at an average of $2.25 per passenger of incremental revenue. Next comes the use of the planes to expose the captive audience to advertising and promotional pitches, including using the outer fuselage of planes as paid billboards. These steps go beyond removing complexity, and may, in fact, add some complexity back to Ryanair's business—for a modest revenue gain. The important point is that the lack of complexity in Southwest's airline business model is its primary appeal because it leads to better transportation service for its traveling customers, which is their primary motive in flying somewhere.

The only airline that is currently a serious threat to Southwest is *Southwest itself.* If it falls prey to the temptation to proliferate routes and other elements of its system in search of growth, it will suffer from the very complexity it has avoided.

The U.S. commercial airline industry is only one example of how companies have added complexity in the quest for growth and market share. Some complexity is inherent in any business. Most of it is introduced with the best of intentions and no idea what the consequences will be. What the airlines got were unmeasured, hidden costs that destroyed profitability. None of the current accounting systems measure these complexity costs, and thus, no one in management recognizes or addresses the causes. The same is happening in computers, but in a different way.

Dell Versus HP

When Dell computer did it differently, using postponement and mass customizations, along with the interactive power of the Internet, to build myriad numbers of computers to match individual customers' wishes, it revolutionized the selling and building of personal computers. And it did so more cost effectively than any one else. This was a "use it" complexity strategy, superbly executed. The reasons this worked are instructive and make a good guideline for others. When a platform design can be used and variations added late in the production/fulfillment cycle, the benefits are large in many areas. Decades before, the Japanese automakers had used a type of business group, called a *keiretsu,* clustering suppliers closely around their production plants, and Dell learned from them. Dell added the dimension of Internet ordering to dramatically reduce lead-time and tighten inventory levels, while being able to rapidly custom-build computers in virtually any configuration a customer might want.

Competitors like HP/Compaq were trapped in a build-to-stock retail model that faced model complexity and component cost deflation, both of which drove costs up, inventories up, and profits down. As PCs have matured and the price-deflation curve has plateaued, HP is enjoying a resurgence, and has overtaken Dell. Growing laptop computer popularity is helping it concentrate on fewer models, each of which include all of the most popular features. (Remember how the Japanese auto companies did this?) Dell, on the other hand, has discovered that volume product categories like servers, printers, etc., with more standardized configurations, do not benefit nearly as much from its mass-customization strategy. This has reduced its relative cost advantage in these highly competitive segments. At times, it is important to realize when complexity works as a strategy and when it no longer works—and needs to be eliminated. Time will tell whether Michael Dell can once again jump-start Dell's growth curve. At Dell, (large) size growth will necessarily come more slowly. Its build-to-order production model is much-less influential in a market that seems to be accepting standard configurations with most of the important features built in.

Larry Ellison's War on Complexity

In 2001 (around the time Theresa Metty was tackling complexity at Motorola), Oracle CEO Larry Ellison was evangelizing about a strategic campaign he called his "war on complexity." In that campaign, Ellison was advising business managers to change the way they thought about business. In particular, he argued against the spending of limited resources on customizing core business applications like ERP (enterprise-resource planning) and CRM (customer-relationship management) to specific needs, because the situations and specifications would inevitably change, driving yet another round of customization, and so on. Oracle's "war on complexity" was intended to reduce the number of specific applications, in favor of tailoring its more robust systems to do what was needed. Ellison's war never got as much traction as he'd have liked, but his idea had great merit, and elements of it are still at work today.

Thus, we have morphed from airplanes to computers to computer software (which you recall, can be structured to handle complex transactions very rapidly). An opportune field for computers to enable a compete-on-complexity strategy is the financial-systems world. Credit-card company Capital One has done a remarkable job with just that kind of strategy, and using computers to make it relatively simple and easy.

Capital One Capitalizes on Complexity

Capital One realized that people don't all want the same kind of credit card. However, its computers and banking network could be designed such that it didn't matter very much what kind of card you wanted, as long as it had included that potential variation in its program structure. Thus, a nearly infinite menu of credit cards—for every user and every situation—was born. This move took the one-size-fits-all competitors like American Express by surprise. This "use it" complexity-based strategy has been widely acknowledged, but still contains many insights. The key insight is the importance of designing the structure and processes such that many variations can be added with little or no systemic or transaction cost.

To use this strategy requires a clear and continuously updated understanding of the choices consumers are making (or might make in the future) in the variety of options a credit card can offer. A combination of discounts on certain types of purchases, no annual fees, low interest rates, balance transfers, rebates, frequent flier miles, affinity affiliations with other companies, and many, many other forms of customization can all fit within a well-designed system such as the one used by Capital One. Then advertising can be shifted as consumer preferences shift, to emphasize "what's hot" and ignore "what's not." This is a good example of an integrated marketing strategy to capitalize on complexity.

Apple-Redux

The latest move by Apple Computer, its changeover to Intel microprocessors, is evidence that it understands the value of competing on complexity in just the right way. By using Intel microprocessors Apple is able to develop hardware and software that permits its users to run either Apple's proprietary OS-X operating system, or the vastly more-common Windows XP operating system from Microsoft. This "killed three birds with one stone." First, it aligns Apple with the leader in microprocessors—Intel. Second, it aligns Apple with the leader in

PC operating systems and software—Microsoft. And third, it permits the small but loyal base of Mac users to crossover into the PC world on those occasions where that's an advantage. Does this add complexity for Apple? Yes, but it's worth the added complexity, since it provides Apple a huge growth opportunity—one that is unparalleled in its recent history.

Using a measured dose of complexity wisely means that Apple gets it right—again. Because it offers a few, well-thought-out and innovative variations of its computers, and a few versions of its blockbuster products like the iPod, it can handle the added complexity while opening up a huge market segment and establishing relationships with the market leaders.

Combine this with the Mac Mini, a full CPU computer for under $700 that uses existing keyboards and monitors, and the newly announced iPhone and Apple TV, and Apple is methodically eliminating the reasons not to switch to a Mac for home and business. *Wall Street Journal* electronics "expert," Walter Mossberg, says it well: "Part of the secret of Apple TV is that, like most of Apple's products, it doesn't try to do everything, and thus become a mess of complexity." No wonder Apple continues to make money in computers and its ingenious (derivative) devices, where others seem to struggle. This is called competing with complexity—"using it" where it matters and "losing it" where it is a disadvantage.

FAST FOOD

"Cheeburger, Cheeburger, Pepsi, Chips": The Advantages of Simplicity

> *"Even if you're on the right track, you'll get run over if you just sit there."*
> —Will Rogers

During the late 1970s, a legendary *Saturday Night Live* TV skit performed by John Belushi and others featured a rowdy, down-to-earth diner that had one kind of meal it knew how to make: "Cheeburger, Pepsi, Chips." Try to order something else and Belushi's counterman would clearly remind you, "No! Cheeburger, Pepsi, chips? Yes?"

Was this funny? Yes! Was it a good idea for a business? Maybe. If the order is for more than one cheeburger, it is repeated, and the grill man knows to put multiple hamburger patties on the grill. Complexity never darkens the door of this diner. Silly? Too simplistic? Maybe not, especially if one considers what the three largest burger sellers in the United States have been through over the past few decades.

The Temptation to Add Choices

McDonald's grew up as the fast-food giant in mass-production America. It cooked burgers by the hundreds, thousands, and ultimately millions—we knew because the signs used to tally how many millions were sold until the numbers just got too big. McDonald's was the Henry Ford of fast food. All regular hamburgers and cheeseburgers were made the same: ketchup, mustard, pickle, and onion, done on an assembly line process next to the grill.

The original McDonald's burger choices were: cheese or no cheese, Coke or shake? (Special orders to omit condiments took longer.) Not quite as simple as Belushi's *SNL* diner, but almost. This kept costs down and facilitated fast production to serve the mealtime rushes with fast service. And this too, like Henry Ford's simplicity strategy, was brilliant for its time. Then things started to change. The temptation to add more choices was irresistible, so along came the Big Mac. At least its basic ingredients were the same, except for the dollop of "special sauce," making the assembly line process work nearly the same. But competition reared its ugly head and more changes were necessary.

Burger King introduced its broiler conveyor belt and told us, "have it your way." It also came up with the Whopper (far bigger than McDonald's burgers), which was assembled to order at the end of the cooking conveyor—"your way." Now the battle was on. McDonald's felt compelled to at least match Burger King with a bigger burger, and the Quarter Pounder was introduced.

Now the assembly line had another platform variable—the size of the hamburger patty and bun were different. Complexity was creeping in. Until then, variations like large and small French fries and large or small Cokes could be done by mass customization as the order was being "picked."

Another competitor, Wendy's, didn't bother with the broiler conveyor, but still used an assemble-to-order method to mass-customize burgers. The purposeful complexity strategy of these two large competitors began to erode McDonald's market share based on its one-kind-fits-all, mass-production model. The drive for variety continued as McDonald's saw the rise of Kentucky Fried Chicken, Taco Bell, Arby's, and many others as fast-food competitors. Wisely, McDonald's decided not to add chicken as a primary menu choice, but instead added a simpler, smaller format that was compatible with its French fry cooking processes—Chicken McNuggets. Still, the McDonald's menu was built around the mass-production model rather than the mass-customization format used by competitors, to which it was losing ground.

McDonald's realized that being open for breakfast presented a good opportunity and came up with another blockbuster product—the Egg McMuffin. This clever concoction included a round fried egg (compatible with the grill), a round piece of Canadian bacon (also simple to warm on the grill), and a toasted English muffin. Add a slightly different special sauce and voilà, you have a poor man's eggs Benedict via mass production, almost exactly parallel to the process for making a cheeseburger.

Complexity at the Heart of the Problem

Over the years, McDonald's continued with many menu changes, additions, missteps, and few successes. Suffice it to say that everything else it added to the menu to combat competitors' offerings added more complexity than profit.

Finally McDonald's restaurants opened closer and closer together and began to cannibalize each other, while more competitors flooded the fast-food field with more and different offerings. After fighting the cooking-system issue for years, the new complexity in the business, and the growth of mass customization in core markets, McDonald's was forced to make a huge change. McDonald's launched its "custom cooking system," a combination of Burger King's cook to order and Wendy's assemble to order. Not only did McDonald's franchisees balk at paying their half of a sizable capital investment, but the bigger issue was learning to use the new system and training employees to use it. This caused McDonald's serious problems, the most vexing of which was that the food no longer came out fast. Complexity had slowed McDonald's to a snail's pace.

At the heart of this matter was the fact that, over the years, McDonald's had layered complexity after complexity on its restaurants but it had not changed the structure, processes, culture, and relationships in a comparable manner. The result was predictable—complexity struck with a vengeance. Food quality sagged, operating costs soared, and orders took longer and longer to complete, clogging both counters and drive-through lanes. When the Complexity Crisis is at the heart of problems, they only yield to changes that address the root cause—*complexity*—not quick fixes.

Fortunately for McDonald's, in a case similar to how the U.S. auto producers all wandered down similar paths until attacked by the Japanese automakers, both Burger King and Wendy's made several of the same mistakes McDonald's made. They attempted to proliferate in order to create growth. Breakfast menus were harder to produce than expected, salad bars created massive amounts of spoilage and sanitation issues, and new menu items proliferated to add sales and costs but not profits. Does this sound familiar? It should. Each fell victim to complexity of one kind or another. Perhaps the ultrasimple "Cheeburger, Pepsi, chips" model was a good idea after all.

TOO MANY OF EVERYTHING?

Brand Proliferation and Line-Extension Can Be Deadly

> "America is a nation that conceives many
> odd inventions for getting somewhere but it
> can think of nothing to do once it gets there."
> —Will Rogers

Twenty-five years ago, Al Ries and Jack Trout wrote a wonderful book: *Positioning: The Battle for Your Mind.* In the book, they describe how creating a clear and simple picture of your product or service in someone's mind is a powerful competitive advantage—a form of differentiation that is difficult for competitors to defeat. They also go on at great length about how foolish proliferation can be, and how overextending a brand can cause much more harm than good. Why? Because the sales revenue splits among new brand extensions; SKUs proliferate, and unless the brand truly expands the market by offering something different (of value), the brand's sales go up only a little, if at all, and profits nearly always go down.

Sounds a lot like the Complexity Crisis, doesn't it? Their premier example was 7UP—"the Uncola," as it was known at one time. The company created a whole series of different line extensions—Diet

7Up, Cherry 7UP, Diet Cherry 7UP, etc.—but 7UP's market share and total sales barely moved. People in that era wanted cola or uncola, and it didn't matter that uncola came in different varieties. The demand was only so great for an alternative to cola.

Too Much Choice Is Worse Than Too Little

This book started off with a reference to the complexity of simply choosing the right telephone service. Dozens of other examples of complexity, and how it afflicts us in everyday life, could have been used. A simple trip to the grocery store, home center, electronics store, or supercenter will tell you all you need to know about how complexity is creating huge inefficiencies in all walks of life. Everything you see on those shelves is some company's nightmare of complexity. The retailer simply pulls it all together and puts it on display.

About 10 percent of the items do about 90 percent of the sales. That's even more skewed than Pareto's 80–20 rule. There will be about 30,000 items, give or take a few in a supermarket these days. Each year, some 10,000 to 20,000 new ones will appear. Some will occupy shelf space briefly and then fail, only to disappear and be found on the manufacturer's financial statements hidden in its variances (to dispose of obsolete packaging), in its inventory (where reserves for obsolescence will have to be increased to cover the write down), and/ or in reduced gross margin (due to the impact of selling closeouts at below-cost pricing).

Do I really need those eighty-five to ninety different kinds of crackers to satisfy my need for the five to seven varieties I buy all the time? Ah, you say, but you might buy one of those new ones and like it. Hope springs eternal in the hearts of marketers. But at the end of the day, doesn't this add meaningless and unnecessary complexity?

Some companies drive complexity back into their suppliers as they hope to hide their competitive-value differences by avoiding direct head-to-head competition on the same items. These companies ask for subbrands and derivative brands, hoping to either confuse or mislead customers about the relative competitiveness of their offerings. They fight and threaten suppliers, each striving to capture exclusive rights to the premier brand, but in the process they drive suppliers crazy and add complexity and hidden cost at every step of the way. Consumers are smarter than marketers think, and often see through this expensive subterfuge.

Some companies proliferate in hopes of blanketing every possible variety under an umbrella brand. Take Tylenol, which was introduced to the market by Johnson and Johnson as a brand of acetaminophen, a pain reliever that is different from aspirin and easier on the stomach. Since cold remedies include a fever reducer, one of Tylenol's attributes, and the Tylenol brand is very well known, there are now numerous Tylenol-branded cold and cough remedies. How many ways can you treat a sniffly nose and a cough? Judging from the neighborhood pharmacy, there are hundreds of ways (but all use almost the same handful of active ingredients). Just walk down the aisle and count the boxes of the well-known brands. Then stop and read the active ingredients to see what is different about them. Complexity runs rampant in dozens of brands. Does it pay to line-extend so extensively until every niche of every segment is covered? No! You are just dividing up the business and multiplying the costs—and that is bad math, with or without the Complexity Factor.

SAME, BUT DIFFERENT

When "Close" Isn't Good Enough—
Two Decades of Evidence

> *"Success is a lousy teacher. It seduces smart people into thinking they can't lose."*
> —Bill Gates

For as long as I have been involved in business, the companies I have worked with have been chasing top-line growth—profitable sales growth—but above all else, growth. Companies around the world still are. As I progressed through a career as an executive and then a consultant, and a member of boards of directors, I began to see this problem again and again. People were nibbling around the edges of it, but not getting at the heart of it. They certainly weren't solving it; if anything, their frantic struggle for growth was making it worse. The realization of how to recognize it, describe it, measure it, and fix it evolved over the past five years. "It" was the Complexity Crisis.

First, let me take you back in time. The bicycle business was a global business long before many others were. That's because bikes are the most efficient, and least costly, form of vehicular transportation to travel greater distances than are suitable for walking, and were adopted early in a society's development.

I was fortunate to be the leader of the largest bike producer in the world from 1983 to 1992, and I learned a lot during that ten-year stretch. One of the most important things I learned was how complexity sneaks up on you when you are seeking growth. We bought bike components all over the world, and chased those suppliers as the industry moved from Europe to Japan to Taiwan/Korea, and finally to China. Each new country was a new development experience where we found new, low-cost suppliers. That was where I first felt effects of the Complexity Crisis.

One of the most-common statements from our Taiwanese vendors when we asked them why they didn't make products exactly to our specifications was, "They are just the same—but different." (Translation: not the same at all.) We learned the danger of that doctrine, and the crippling complexity it adds when we sold bikes to our North American neighbors (Canada and Mexico), and thus (mistakenly), assumed that selling them in Europe and Asia would be easy—after all, it would be "just the same, but different." Mexico and Canada required multilingual owner's manuals, but everything else about the product was the same as the U.S. version.

As Toys "R" Us expanded globally, it took our bicycles as part of its merchandise assortment, to enhance the "American mystique" of its stores. More and more Toys "R" Us stores opened in Europe and Asia, so we decided we'd make bikes to sell in Europe and Asia. Since we were selling to Toys "R" Us, we thought selling to the other major retailers in those countries should be easy too. After all, a bike is a bike, isn't it?

The answer was "almost, but not quite." The structure—the frame, fork, wheels, etc.—was essentially the same, but that was where the similarity ended. Much to our chagrin, we discovered that each new country we sold to had some dissimilarity that required a unique model variation.

In Japan, there was a restriction on the width of bike handlebars. This meant different handlebars—a different part number, bill of materials, model number—for every bike we sold in Japan. And yes, the owner's manual had to be translated into Japanese too—and then printed in small quantities for each different kind of bike—driving up the cost and exposing us to risks of obsolescence whenever we made changes. British bikes had the caliper-brake levers on opposite sides of the bike handlebars. Why did that surprise us? After all, they drive on the "wrong side of the road" there. German bikes required attachments for a generator set because the bikes are often ridden after dark, thus requiring lights—a practice we discourage in the United States for safety reasons. Spanish law requires each bike to contain a unique identifier—a homologation number—via a nonremovable marking. Then we learned that "Mexican Spanish" was different from the Spanish spoken in Spain. It wasn't a lot different, but just different enough—"same, but different." The "Canadian French" was a little different from French spoken in France, too. That meant every country so far needed a unique model for one reason or another. The differences were individually minor, but in the aggregate, it doubled the number of models.

When we looked at standard costs of the different models, they weren't much different from the domestic model from which they were derived. Somehow, we realized later, *these costs were hidden.* Complexity drove up our costs dramatically, increased assembly line training time, and required smaller purchase quantities and shorter production runs, leading to more frequent changeovers—all to produce European/Asian bike models. But *nothing* in our standard-cost systems captured those costs; they disappeared into unidentified (and unfavorable) expenses in variances or overhead accounts. Standards were developed for the assortment we usually ran, and overhead was allocated across departments and families of products (as was SG&A). The impact of complexity went undetected.

Then we got the big surprise. Profit margins went down. Quality suffered. Service levels slipped. This was a surprise, considering that these were nearly identical to the bikes we ran by the thousands day in and day out. That was just it, though—they were *almost the same, but not exactly the same*—thus, they were different. In hindsight we should have seen what was happening. Of course, our metrics should have tracked it, but nobody recognized the Complexity Crisis back then. There were no metrics—and still aren't—to track complexity. That didn't matter because growth was the mantra of that era.

What started out to be an exciting new piece of business turned into a big, complex project, with lots of risk and more hidden costs than we ever imagined. Not only that, but other issues arose as well. If a U.S. bike was boxed with incorrect components or instructions, it was a Consumer Product Safety Commission–reportable problem. We might even have to recall the bike if it was a safety hazard. We knew how to deal with that, and it was seldom an issue. However, we now had to understand it in seven new countries.

A solution for our owner's manuals was to "simply" do what electronics companies did—print in multiple languages. The problem was that the many illustrations, safety warnings, etc. our manuals contained made them too long—sixty-five pages—and expensive to produce in 5-plus languages. We'd be inserting a veritable telephone-book-size manual in the bikes' packaging. Standardizing manuals for 200,000 European/Asian bikes meant incurring that extra cost of a big, thick manual in 4 million U.S. bikes.

Complexity had us firmly in its grasp and backing out was painful, if not downright impractical. The only choice was to develop the structures, processes, culture, and relationships to manage our self-induced complexity—while we suffered its adverse effects.

In company after company, I found a similar misunderstanding of the consequences of using proliferation to chase sales growth. Slowly, but surely, a pattern began to emerge and I realized what needed to be done.

Same, But Different—Circa Early 1990

When I arrived at Rubbermaid Office Products Group in 1992, I found a huge product line—over 4,000 SKUs scattered among nine business units on four continents. It had grown out of mergers, acquisitions, and the search for growth by selling more of everything to everybody, everywhere.

Service was terrible, but it should have been no surprise that trying to fill orders for hundreds of products from as many as ten DCs (distribution centers) was an obvious problem of complexity. There were about a dozen shades of beige desk accessories and wastebaskets, all of which were very similar. These had grown insidiously over the preceding years as Rubbermaid and Eldon, its merger partner, had matched their products to the colors of the major office-furniture makers. This was clearly a good idea, right? When Steelcase or Herman Miller or Hon introduced a new shade of beige, so did Eldon-Rubbermaid (as it was called for a while). But because the office furniture had a long life, the older colors had to be retained too. The furniture manufacturers, of course, never wanted their "beige" to match the one of their competitors. Then every year or two, a marketing product manager wanted a new beige color, too, to sell to the mass market, and it clearly had to be different than the ones sold to the upscale markets. Additions were continuous, deletions were rare or never. People in the plant and distribution center, and even contract molders, kept getting the colors confused because they were so similar.

I finally challenged the sales and marketing group to help address this problem. We laid out letter trays molded in all of the "beige colors" on a large conference table, in a sort of graded color scale, with nearly alike colors next to each other. The color identifiers were marked on the bottom by coded numbers. A stack of index cards with each color's "true name" was also stacked on the table. *If* the sales and marketing people could correctly match the names with the colors, they could keep all of them. If they couldn't, half were to be eliminated and substitutions decided upon. They failed the matching test, and half of the colors were phased out, with inventory to be used up.

The apprehension the sales group felt when they told distributors (customers) about the change turned to a strange sort of happiness. The distributors were delighted. They hated having to carry so many nearly identical products and were afflicted with the same complexity-related problems of added inventory, confusion in distribution, etc.

As far as the matching of accessories to furniture, the consolidation was never mentioned. The color variations in paint, different furniture/desktop materials, and the molding-resin shades, combined with fading due to age and UV exposure, meant nobody even noticed the change—except our planning group.

Using a combination of such approaches, during a fifteen-month period, the number of SKUs was reduced from 4,000+ to just over 1,000, inventory turns more than doubled, and a massive amount of obsolete and noncurrent inventory was eliminated. This permitted DCs to be reduced to three, then to two, and finally to one, just over a year later. Profits in the business doubled on modest (8–9 percent) growth in sales.

Same, but Different, in the Twenty-First Century

Not many years later, as a board member at Amrep, a leading chemical formulator and packager for the automotive, janitorial, and industrial markets, I saw complexity strike again. Amrep made a deal with a large customer to acquire its captive private-label line of chemicals, close a plant, and consolidate production into an existing plant with open capacity. That's a good kind of deal—right? Not quite. The assumption was that the formulas were "almost the same" as current products and the volume would be a nice incremental addition. Wrong. Complexity struck again, disguised as "just the same, but different."

Once again, we learned that "close, almost, and nearly" are not the same as "exactly." The products were intended to do very similar jobs, but over the years, each company had evolved to its own unique formulas, which were all different—just a little. Thus the SKUs (mixtures) to be produced nearly doubled. The same situation described in the Huffy story developed. Runs had to be cut short and mixtures reformulated more often. Purchase volumes for containers were different and lower, so costs were higher. Employees became confused and mixed up the contents and the containers. EPA permits had to be revised or rewritten. Inventories grew and service levels dropped, as did profitability.

Only after the problem was recognized did some tough discussions with the customer begin. The formulas were standardized and the number reduced to drive out complexity so the plant was able to resume effective production. The revenue growth added by taking on a simple capacity filler of "almost the same" products created havoc for months. When unnecessary complexity was eliminated, productivity climbed and overtime dropped dramatically. If the customer demanded unique formulations, they were priced based on the actual purchase volumes and run sizes. Ultimately, the customer shopped the business elsewhere (since the formulas were now standardized) and much of it was spread among several different suppliers. Conquering complexity solved one problem but left its scars on the business. Nonetheless, this lost business was the unprofitable part that was being subsidized by the profitable customers.

In each case, we found complexity embedded so deeply in the growth struggle that it was hard to separate. The same lesson, learned over and over, is one that you don't have to re-enact to learn. Complexity strikes unseen or unnoticed and it hits costs, quality, service, asset utilization, and perhaps most damaging of all, it occupies huge portions of managerial time that could be put into new, profitable opportunities. Close is not good enough. The phrase "almost the same" means "different." Perhaps worst of all, it consumes the valuable resources of the victim company—people, time, and money—denying the ability to focus on real growth opportunities.

Industries May Vary but the Complexity Crisis Hits Them All

Most of the examples thus far have dealt with product businesses. The principles of the Complexity Factor and the "use it or lose it" strategy are equally applicable to hotels, restaurants, service businesses, and so on. The primary variable is how to define a product SKU and a served market. Once that is resolved, like companies can readily benchmark their progress using their own calculated Complexity Factor and the other metrics discussed. The principles are exactly the same—and so are the outcomes.

The Complexity Crisis lies in wait, silently siphoning profits from companies in many industries unless they understand what it does, and how it affects them. Forewarned is forearmed. Understand which of the variations add complexity and which can be readily handled incrementally without adding much (or any?) complexity within the chosen structure and processes. Realize how these variations will have to be managed and the effects on people, the culture, and their external-relationship partners. Once that is clearly understood, then decisions about whether to use it or lose it, and how, will become much easier

Parallels exist in virtually every type of industry. Choosing whether to deal with the Complexity Crisis by a use-it or a lose-it strategy is a critical decision for everyone, in every company. Finding the right cost and pricing model to get paid for the level of complexity versus the competition is also a critical strategic step. Once those decisions are made, then the changes in the structure, processes, culture, and relationships can be made. Realignment and restructuring, total or partial, may be necessary depending on which decision is to be implemented. Once complexity has been identified, controlled, and driven out, companies must be vigilant to preclude the possibility that complexity creeps back into the business in the wrong strategic way. Even when the decision is to compete using complexity, this is a big challenge.

SCIENCE VERSUS BUSINESS

The Scientific Version of Complexity

"Expansion means complexity and complexity decay."
—C. Northcote Parkinson, British historian and author

For those who would say that any book on complexity cannot overlook the powerful learning from natural science, I am including a layman's perspective of how scientists perceive complexity. There are many lessons to be learned from nature and science. Some are metaphors with business parallels. Others are genuine insights into how business might act or evolve given certain stimuli. As companies become increasingly complex, they temporarily generate some surprisingly good economic results. Then, they often tumble into wasteful chaos, and results decline. Only after a protracted period of time, and usually external intervention, does the chaos begin to once again resolve itself into order. In science and in business, for a short time, complexity can yield some amazing results; but left unchecked, complexity will tumble into chaos, out of which order's emergence will be far too random and slow. The classic example of this is how a company expands too fast (remember the dot-coms), yielding great results for a short time, then the company loses control (falls into chaos) and cannot sustain the growth-related complexity. As it tries to regain control (and not stay in chaos), it cannot. The business result is filing chapter 11, the bankruptcy proceeding that "freezes" things and allows reorganization. In nature, there is no chapter 11. Time is required for order to emerge from chaos and the unsuited species/organisms simply cease to exist.

There are meaningful parallels between the words "complexity" as I use it throughout this book and the scientific term "complexity" used by serious biological scientists.

As far back as the late 1980s, Heinz Pagels wrote in *The Dreams of Reason*, "I am convinced that the nations and people who master the new science of complexity will become the economic, cultural, and political superpowers of the next century." This is a very powerful statement, but one that bears further scrutiny.

WHAT DOES "COMPLEXITY" REALLY MEAN?

As Heinz Pagels writes: "What is complexity? Up until now we have been using the term 'complexity' rather loosely to convey what it means in ordinary language—it refers to a state of affairs that has many interacting, different components. Now it is time to move beyond that loose definition. Complexity . . . is a quantitative measure that can be assigned to a physical system or a computation that lies midway between the measure of simple order and complete chaos. . . . Complexity thus covers a vast territory that lies between order and chaos."

About ten years ago, I became involved with some of the leading biological scientists in the quest for knowledge about this emerging field of study—complexity and chaos. I met Stuart Pimm at the University of Tennessee, where we discussed his studies of ecosystems, from which one can easily draw analogies to markets in the field of business. Complexity theory and the study of natural ecosystems leads one to believe that a given ecosystem, like a given market in business, can only support a finite number of species, or in the business sense, competitors. If there are too many occupants competing for the same spaces and resources, Darwinian survival theories then come into play and the strong defeat the weak, thus reducing the number of competitors.

Stuart Pimm then introduced me to Stuart Kauffman, one of the world's leading scientists, and author of a landmark book in this field, *Origins of Order*. I met with Kauffman in his Santa Fe, New Mexico, home to discuss the parallels between complexity theory in his world (science) and in mine (business). I also spoke with author Roger Lewin, whose fine book, *Complexity: Life at the Edge of Chaos,* helped educate me on how complexity in the natural world has parallels in our business world. In Lewin's book, Chris Langton, a member of the Santa Fe Institute, used vivid terms to describe how he saw complexity using a blackboard: "Totally ordered over here. . . . Totally random over here. Complexity happens somewhere in between. . . . The science of Complexity has to do with structure and order."

For most laymen, the terms "chaos" and "complexity" mean almost the same thing, but not so for serious scientists. In simplistic terms, order reigns, albeit with increasing complexity, until it falls over the boundary into chaos. If left to itself, chaos will return to some kind of order again. The problem is that this takes time to happen. In the business world, the company could be long gone before the tumble from complexity to chaos finds its way back to a semblance of order. Scientists often refer to these kinds of systems as "self-organizing." I have encountered some self-organizing efforts in the business world, and on occasion, they work pretty well.

Some might say that the chapter 11 reorganization in bankruptcy is a way for businesses to buy time and seek a return from chaos to order. The key is to head off this outcome—to recognize the growth of complexity and stop short of tumbling over the edge into chaos. Scientists believe that the highly complex boundary between complexity and chaos is a place where small inputs can lead to large changes. That could be construed to mean it is a place where there is a lot of leverage, where small inputs/changes can create large outputs/changes, and in many respects that also is true. Perhaps this is particularly true for business, but if the large changes are in the wrong direction, watch out. There will be no chance to wait for order to re-emerge; here comes chapter 7—liquidation!

The continuing evolution of species in their respective ecosystems also leads to interesting quasi-business conclusions. The most interesting of these is what biologists call "the Red Queen effect," named by Leigh Van Valen of the University of Chicago as resonant of Alice in *Through the Looking Glass*. The predator and prey species have to keep running hard just to stay in the same relative place. There are those scientists (biologists) who contend that the Red Queen is the primary force behind evolutionary history.

Stuart Kauffman is quoted in Lewin's book as saying it this way:

You see it with technological innovation in industrial societies, too. Think of the first bicycles or the first cars. Lots of experimentation to begin with, different forms of bicycle, different forms of propulsion and design for cars, or whatever you're thinking of, the extremes get weeded out, a few forms survive, and subsequent innovation focuses on improvement on the remaining themes.

Stuart Pimm also weighed in on his perspective when talking to Roger Lewin, offering a viewpoint he reiterated in our conversations: "The new science of Complexity might be relevant to nature, to the important patterns of biology. . . . Isn't much of ecology based on the idea of simple equilibria, and that the behavior of species in ecosystems is predictable in that kind of framework?" To which I said, "Isn't much of business competition based on the idea of simple balances in the marketplace (equilibria) and the behavior of competitors (species) in markets (ecosystems) predictable in that kind of framework?" Do you see the parallels? Pimm, Lewin, and Kauffman speak in scientific terms, but we can "hear" them in business terms if we just listen closely. The parallels are all there. Complexity in science, while technically different from the complexity described in this book, isn't all that different in its effects.

Let's try to wrap this up with some concluding lessons from science on how complexity impacts business. In science, the area of complexity just before the tumble into chaos is very productive—temporarily. Scientific complexity theory, liberally translated, tells us that once complexity has fallen into chaos, order will emerge from that chaos—given time. But in business, we often cannot wait for this to happen. So we keep "doing things," trying to hurry what cannot be hurried. Businesses introduce complexity when trying to grow faster than the markets permit. They do so without recognizing the implications of their actions until too late. As complexity increases, first the results get better, and then suddenly, they tumble into chaos, and the results get dramatically worse. (Remember the dot-coms?) Panic stricken, we seek complex solutions and by doing so make our problems more complex than they were initially. Nature solves this by letting species die off and become extinct—only the fittest survive—after the emergence from chaos. In business, this isn't a very attractive option, although in some industries it is what's needed (airlines, for one example). Thus we try to "manage" out of the chaos. My purpose in including this scientific parallel is to illustrate how much better it would have been to control and contain the complexity in the first place. There are many lessons for business that can be learned by studying nature. This metaphor provides one of the most profound lessons about complexity.

PART THREE

The Solutions

STRATEGIES AND SOLUTIONS

What Can You Do about Complexity?

"The first step to getting the things you want out of life is this: Decide what you want."
—Ben Stein, actor, writer, and academic

The most common cause of management-induced complexity is the constant striving of companies to achieve high growth in low-growth markets. They struggle; they stretch; they create more new products; enter new markets; expand distribution; add facilities and staff; expand systems—all the while adding complexity at a far greater rate than revenue or profits.

The more possibilities managers see, the more proliferation they create in blind hopes of finding some sort of competitive advantage and the profitability that goes with it. Add to that the complexity of globalization, outsourcing, fragmented and transient work forces, and the increased use of temporary employees or contractors and the challenges become even more complex. The purpose of any company should not be to stifle growth through innovation. It should be to make it productive and profitable.

The Difference Between Creativity and Innovation

The key objective is to find complexity if it exists and decide whether to keep it and use it as a competitive weapon, or to eliminate it and the hidden costs it is creating. This does not mean stifling innovation. It does mean understanding that creativity, and the proliferation it can create, is not the same as innovation. Consider the following beliefs of the late Theodore Leavitt, one of the leading marketing thinkers and authors of the twentieth century and a longtime professor at the Harvard Business School, in his article "Creativity Is Not Enough":

> Creativity is often touted as a miraculous road to organizational growth and affluence. But creative new ideas can hinder rather than help a company if they are put forward irresponsibly. Too often, the creative types who generate a proliferation of ideas confuse creativity with practical innovation. Without understanding the operating executive's day-to-day problems or the complexity of business organizations, they usually pepper their managers with intriguing but short memoranda that lack details about what's at stake or how the new ideas should be implemented. They pass off onto others the responsibility for getting down to brass tacks. . . . Extolling corporate creativity at the expense of conformity may, in fact, reduce the creative animation of business. Conformity and rigidity are necessary for corporations to function.

There is a way to use creativity and complexity where it yields a strategic competitive advantage. Instead of driving out complexity, reducing SKUs, customers, markets, etc. (the "lose it" strategy), a company can profitably compete on complexity as a differentiator. This must be accomplished by designing the company's structure, processes, and culture to capitalize on complexity, using it to create customization for individuals and groups of customers, where those customers value customization and will pay appropriately for it (the "use it" strategy). Here is a framework for thoughts about which strategic direction to choose and how to proceed with the right approach for your business.

Innovation Versus Complexity

In their 2005 *Harvard Business Review* article titled the same as the heading of this section, Mark Gottfredson and Keith Aspinall of consultancy Bain and Company make several important points. The focus of their approach is to decide how much innovation is appropriate before it leads to needless or damaging complexity. The term they use is "finding the innovation fulcrum"—the pivot point where innovation suddenly tips over into complexity.

Such an analysis must necessarily deal with two issues:

- The amount of innovation
- The speed or frequency of innovation

Both can cause either great success or immense turmoil. The way Gottfredson and Aspinall put it is: "the pursuit of innovation can be taken too far. As a company increases the pace of innovation, its profitability often begins to stagnate or even erode. The reason can be summed up in one word: complexity. The continual launch of new products and line extensions adds complexity throughout a company's operations, and, as the costs of managing that complexity multiply, margins shrink."

Misguided innovation not only causes margins to shrink, but also causes the bottom line to shrink even faster as hidden costs are created in overheads, SG&A, and other expense categories. Few of these problems will be attributed to the innovation initiatives, but the causes can be tracked directly to proliferation and complexity. In fact, Gottfredson and Aspinall admit that this is true: "Managers aren't blind to the problem. Nearly 70% admit that excessive complexity is raising their costs and hindering their profit growth, according to a 2005 Bain survey of more than 900 global executives. What managers often miss is the true source of the problems—the way complexity begins in the product line and then spreads outward through every facet of a company's operations."

This is an insightful observation but the practical question remains, "Why aren't they doing something to measure it, track it, and contain it—or conversely, to use it for competitive advantage?" Admission of the problem with no corresponding solution won't save your organization from complexity creep—and diminished profits and productivity.

The Bain authors start at the right point, but since their goal as consultants is to address innovation, they stop short of executing the solution(s). They say, "The usual antidotes to complexity miss their mark because they treat the problem on the factory floor rather than at the source: in the product line."

The answer to this vexing question starts with a single phrase: clarity of focus. If a company is to contain the growth of complexity without stifling innovation, it must have a crystal-clear focus on how it wishes to compete, and what it must do to succeed in that approach. Complexity is a messy problem to clean up after the fact. Like capturing quality defects via inspection instead of prevention, the crime has already been committed, and all that is possible is damage control.

Few Resources Available; Total Solutions Needed

No one seems to be addressing the problem of complexity in its totality and in the context of the whole business. Studying it is not the same as dealing with it. Other efforts help, but like fixing a flat tire on a car with a wheel missing, they reduce the problems but don't solve the important ones. Unfortunately, in many organizations today, analysis seems to always stop short of the call to action and the roadmap for execution.

Moreover, "solutions" often play to consultants and managers specific expertise; for example, lean, six sigma, process design, or other initiatives-du-jour. That's not necessarily bad. These are powerful programs that can make a sizable impact, but once again, they focus on individual parts of the problem, and in doing so, address/fix only those parts of the problem. To leave parts of complexity untreated is like removing part of a cancer—it will simply regrow and reattack.

By reading the first half of *The Complexity Crisis*, you can understand the scope of the problems and opportunities created by complexity and decide what to do. In the sections that follow I'll provide useful mental models for how a manager and an organization can recognize, think about, measure, diagnose, and take action on the issues of complexity—and whether to lose it or to use it—and what, exactly, those decisions mean. Before leaving this topic, I feel compelled to describe a common problem encountered in business today. It may lead to complexity and always leads to trouble. Once exposed, this problem can often be avoided or at least mitigated.

Beware of Devastating Success

Most companies are very careful in pricing a new sales program. The costs are carefully calculated. The selling prices are diligently negotiated.

Even the mix of products is factored into the calculations. The gross-profit margin is calculated to three decimal places.

If the company has a vigilant financial person pricing the program, costs for extra-payment terms and cash discounts are factored into the profitability analysis. In today's intensive supply chain and sophisticated logistics management, freight costs are also considered.

The lead salesperson and the team are enthused. The big deal is nearly done. It will add huge volume that has been sought after for years. Getting this business will also drive a stake into the heart of a competitor. Everything is great, right? Well, not exactly!

The deal is all set to go forward. Only a few minor details remain to be resolved, and no one, from the CEO on down to the account exec, will let these minor details get in the way of the big sale. But maybe they should. This company could be on the verge of a "devastating success."

There are more costs in a deal than traditional measures capture. If these costs go unnoticed and unquantified, several months after the big sale, and maybe sooner, everyone notices the company doing more volume and making less money. It is also using more assets, and thus earning an even worse return on assets. What happened?

Here are a few examples of actual scenarios that cause such catastrophes. The first is a company selling to a major retailer. The second is a business-to-business industrial situation. Both have one thing in common—more volume, less profits, and even worse returns on assets. When going after the big sale, there is usually excess capacity to be filled, which partly motivates the sales effort. Seldom does the big sale exactly fit the open capacity. In many cases, it exceeds the available capacity by a wide margin, but since it was the big sale, this new business takes precedence over old business.

The new business, because of the volume, carries lower prices and longer payment terms than the old business. It also has a requirement for rapid delivery that is tighter and requires carrying more inventory. Don't say, "You will make it up in volume." Those are the seven words often heard just before a company's financial decline begins.

With slower payment and higher inventories for the big customer squeezing out volume from older customers, who paid faster and accepted slightly slower deliveries (and thus could live with lower inventory levels), working-capital needs go up significantly. Profits are down because more capacity is tied up with lower-margin business. The net result—much lower return on assets. And, you haven't gotten to the cost of the minor details that were required to seal the big deal.

In the retail setting, there are the "buy-back" and closeout sales of competitor's goods currently on the shelf, in order to make room for yours. Then there are the new signage and point-of-purchase display materials not figured in the cost of the deal. Of course, as the new big supplier, there are also the requisite new-store opening freebies and the extra advertising allowances (over what was anticipated in the deal) to give the new product line a worthy launch. After all, you don't want the new line to fail or to deliver reduced sales after closing the big deal.

Perhaps there are a few other costs that creep in, like increased deductions because of a few bugs in the part-numbering systems conversion (or just the fact that the customer's distribution system is unfamiliar with your products, packaging, or markings and rejects or returns several shipments). All together, these "minor details" can wipe out all of the first year's profit on the "big deal" and even eat into year two's profits. This is just about the time that the competitor launches an attack to recover the lost business—requiring you to lower prices to hold the "big volume" or respond to competitive pressure at another large customer.

Perhaps the industrial situation is better—but don't believe it. Mega-customers and their demands come in all industries. The working capital escalation described earlier is applicable in this situation too. Next is the annual 3 percent cost-reduction requirement. Then come the minor details. Waive the minimum setup charge or small-quantity-premium policy. Tighten the spec just a little on one or two key criteria.

And, by the way, with the big deal come a handful of low-volume, nuisance items that are needed to "fill out the line." No one makes money on these "dogs." Add in some expedited delivery costs because of last-minute spec changes or production-schedule shifts, and any profit is again postponed until the second year of the big deal. By then, new technology and new designs are popping up like weeds after a spring rain.

Just remember: You can and must figure every cost of the deal. In my companies, I actually had software developed to make sure we did. Oh well, you had the big deal for a while. Maybe it didn't put you under; it just ate up all of your line of credit, so you can't invest in new process equipment or the needed plant expansion. For that one brief, fleeting moment when you signed the big deal, you were on top of the world. But you know there is only one direction to go once you are on top of the world and that is down. Beware of the devastating success that puts you on top—briefly—before the long fall.

A FIVE-STEP FRAMEWORK FOR THOUGHT

Organized Thinking Reaches Valid Conclusions

> "It must be considered that there is nothing more difficult to carry out, nor more doubtful of success, nor more dangerous to handle, than to initiate a new order of things."
> —Niccolò Machiavelli

When tackling any complex problem, it's helpful to have a framework for thought, lest you lose your way in this tangle of complexity. The best framework for thought follows a sequence through five distinct, but related, dimensions of a business—purpose, structure, processes, relationships, and culture. It is within those dimensions of the business that the strategy and executional foundation resides.

TAC #7: THE FRAMEWORK FOR THOUGHT

- Purpose
- Structure
- Processes
- Relationships
- Culture

Purpose—Why Does the Business Exist?

Every business has a purpose. The only question is whether the founders remember and the employees know what it is, why it is that, and how it got that way. In the business infancy, someone decided that there was a need that could be fulfilled, and thus a business was created to serve a customer. As time went on, this evolved into serving many customers, and if the founder was true to the purpose that caused the business to begin, it likely grew and prospered. The wise founder took the time to decide, "Just what is the purpose of this business?" If it was recorded, tested, communicated, and sustained, then the purpose fulfilled the first dimension of the business. It answers these questions: Why do you deserve to be in business? What do you do that is better than the competing alternatives? Who do you serve? Why and how? I think you see that the purpose is both the cornerstone and the compass for the business. Once it is set, it should remain, largely unchanged, until or unless there is a formidable need to alter it.

Structure—How Are You Set Up and Organized?

The next step in the thought framework is what kind of structure the business needs. To create value, which is the key to creating and keeping customers, a business must have a structure that is consistent with its strategy and vice versa. The structure must reinforce its reason for being—to serve its customers. The term "structure" means how it is set up, organized, and configured.

The structure is made up of people organized to work together in specific configurations, in particular places, and in carefully chosen facilities and infrastructure. Where are they? How many, how big are they? What's done where, by whom, and how and why—and is that appropriate (or necessary)? These are all key structural issues. Just how much change and complexity there should be, and how rapidly the change comes, are key decision factors in choosing the structure.

Structure decisions are usually longer-term considerations and are harder to change quickly, at least without serious pain (e.g., closing facilities, firing people, liquidating assets, etc.). Structural decisions must be made with strategic intent. Obviously, the planned complexity of the company has a dramatic effect on structural decisions. The insidious kinds of structural changes caused by unrecognized complexity can add huge costs to a business without it realizing the cause-and-effect connection.

Distant sales offices or distribution centers are created to serve new or different customers or markets. Groups for tracking and hedging foreign-exchange fluctuations are created to deal with international monetary issues. The creation of organizational units to manage the many issues that come with imports from faraway countries is a logical new structural addition to manage sprawling supply chains.

The problem, however, is that few managers or executives connect the need for such structural parts to a cause of complexity—products, customers, suppliers, markets, and services—each of which made sense by itself, but now conspire to create a tangled web of problems and costs that spin out of control. No one did anything malicious or overtly wrong; the Complexity Crisis is caused by the over-reaching desire to grow by creating and selling more of everything, everywhere, to everyone—a noble cause with devastating effects. Sales go up and profits go down.

Processes—How Does Your Company Do Things?

All companies have processes. When the company is smaller and simpler, so are the processes. Processes are how things get done, and the most important process is the one that serves the customer. As the company grows, the structure grows/evolves and the processes spread like the tentacles of a vine. Circumstances often change rapidly and in unexpected ways, and these changes may render old processes inefficient, obsolete, or dysfunctional. Process-mapping exposes waste, delay, and inefficiency, and sometimes it exposes imminent risks of total breakdown as well. Process-mapping may also reveal a huge amount of unrecognized and unplanned complexity. It is important that the processes support the chosen strategy. Old, overgrown, and inefficient processes will create massive complexity, even if the remainder of the business is successful at resisting unnecessary complexity.

Retailing provides a striking example of how process changes are required to keep up with competition, to contain complexity, and to monitor the profitability of products offered for sale. The huge, growing, and frequently changing mix of products (SKUs) offered by retailers presents a continuing complexity versus profitability balancing act.

A typical retail process problem is that activity-based costing (ABC), which is widely used to estimate the net landed cost of an individual SKU, still is, in fact, an estimate. It uses averages and percentages spread across product groups and is often allocated to sales volume in monetary terms, instead of actual unit product movement. Why is this done? Because it is mathematically simpler and provides the comfort that the retailer is doing SKU analysis and rationalization (even if done on an erroneous basis). This happens in far more than retail markets, but this familiar product example makes it simpler to understand.

Consider a high-volume SKU such as Kraft Macaroni & Cheese, which moves in pallet loads, is an efficient shape to utilize both shelf (retail) and warehouse cubes, and turns quickly. Compare this to another potential Kraft item, say a niche product such as broccoli soup, which must be broken from pallets to cases, reconsolidated to move to stores, and moves much more slowly at retail. Averages and dollar-spread allocations will seldom capture the dramatic difference between the handling costs and velocity of these two items.

Another problem is how the quest for sales growth impacts complexity and then profitability. An Acorn report cites an organization whose sales-growth target was an amazing 300 percent over a three-year period—and it was achieved, but absent other controls. In fact, sales revenues actually grew by 325 percent, but expenses (and that is just the ones they could track accurately) grew even more—337 percent. The result was a negative profit growth on an exciting, high-growth item. What causes could have been identified for expenses climbing more than revenues? There were several identified: increased rebates, smaller and more frequent deliveries, more product variety in the line, and much greater time spent on customer communications. Was this surprising? Yes and no. The cause, of course, was increased complexity.

Remember the devastating success example? This is a similar case where the negative effects of complexity are at work. In the haste to find top-line sales growth, the process redesign phase is often shortcut or skipped entirely. The penalties for this kind of shortcut are large.

In an unrelated industry, a similar growth-related complexity problem is what struck Jet Blue in early 2007. Growth and complexity outpaced processes and systems development, and bad weather did the rest. Like innovation, successful growth also has its complexity-related challenges.

On the other hand, if the strategy had been to create and then compete on high variety, the business processes could have been re-designed to support that approach, and the costs incurred would have been controlled along the way. Pricing and profitability would both have benefited from using the right processes for the strategic approach.

Perhaps Gottfredson and Aspinall offer the most common reason and the most reasonable excuse for such behaviors:

> It's natural for businesses to add products to keep customers happy. Smart marketers have no trouble justifying each addition as a means of adding or protecting revenues. But as more products are added, the costs of the resulting complexity begin to outweigh the revenues, and profits start falling. From that point on, every new offering—however attractive in isolation—just thins margins further. The more aggressively the company innovates in product development, the weaker its results become. . . . What makes the problem particularly damaging is that it tends to be invisible to management.

They go on to confirm the exact premise of the Complexity Crisis. Traditional financial systems simply do not track the links between product proliferation and complexity costs, because the costs are usually product specific. There are many other costs of complexity that extend far beyond those assigned to the products. Those only show up in aggregate expense-account areas such as overheads (associated with managing increasingly complex arrays of products and distribution) and SG&A (the systems and accounting complexity of more transactions involving more products and customers but yielding little or no more revenue). In Peter Drucker's classic *Harvard Business Review* article that I referenced earlier, he points out that costs are largely transaction driven and revenues and profits are volume driven. Having the processes to deal with this profound truth is critical to succeeding in the face of The Complexity Crisis.

Relationships and Culture—How Do You Work Together and With Others?

How people inside a company deal with each other is usually mirrored in their relationships with those outside the company. To conquer complexity—or to use it for competitive advantage—one of the key ingredients is organizational trust and openness. If people inside the company don't trust one another, they won't work together effectively, and that adds unproductive complexity and gets in the way of planned, strategic complexity. The same goes for relationships with the outside organizations—customers, suppliers, consultants, etc. Today's information technology and the Internet make it possible for organizations to share information openly and instantaneously—if they trust each other. High-trust cultures can capitalize on processes designed to use complexity and customization as a powerful competitive differentiator. Low trust usually means less sharing of information and less-transparent communications, both of which inhibit customization strategies and add unproductive complexity.

Almost a decade ago, in an article in *Supply Chain Management Review*, I wrote of the barriers to progress in supply chain and logistics management. These were not technology shortfalls; they were trust shortfalls—human obstacles. More complexity means more work for everyone. There is less time to communicate, less time to be polite, and less time to be tolerant of others errors and oversights. Organizations morph into complex matrix structures trying to manage complexity while maintaining professional expertise and customer orientation. Relationships are strained both inside and outside the company. Suppliers and service providers also reel under the variety, speed, and complexity of demands on them. What started as an exciting ride on the roller coaster becomes a scary, stressful one. Thus, complexity also drives organizational stress.

Contrasting strategies of lose it and use it take two different approaches. Trying to serve two masters with such different needs is tough on an organization's mindset and culture. In the former, complexity is driven out, and simplification and efficiency are used to reduce hidden costs. This requires one sort of culture—one of simplicity. Obviously, certain customers, markets, and segments are more willing to buy from a supplier of goods or services using this approach. Pricing will normally be lower in these segments, and volumes may be higher.

In the use it approach to embracing complexity, the systems, structure, processes, technology, and culture are intended to consciously capture customers through variety, customization, and intentional proliferation. This approach can be a powerful competitive tool if it is managed well, but it puts different stresses on the company's culture and relationships (with suppliers, for example). It is powerful because it allows competing customers to have uniquely different offerings (e.g., home-improvement chains like Home Depot and Lowe's prefer to avoid head-to-head competition on exactly the same brands and items). It allows individual customers (or consumers) to choose different features and benefits that are customized to meet their needs (e.g., Capital One offers myriad credit cards with different programs; Dell offers customized computers to match the desires of its online customers.) But this is far easier to describe than to execute; it takes strong advance planning and firm discipline in execution.

Finding the right balance of pricing versus the cost of execution is a critical step. Transactions, for one example, must be highly systematized so that the costs of individualizing them are almost insignificant. This means thinking in advance of all the variations the system must accommodate. Dell Computer largely mastered this approach to custom-build computers at rapid delivery cycles. Unfortunately, it stubbed its toe on off-shoring its after-sale service because the wide product-configuration variety made for a nearly infinite number of unique problems to diagnose and solve. This was difficult with a far-away, less-competent customer-service work force. When choosing the option of using complexity as a competitive tool, it is wise to think through its many future implications before committing to that path.

COMPLEXITY'S IMPACT ON ORGANIZATIONS

How It Can Drive Them Crazy

"Work expands so as to fill the time available for its completion."
—C. Northcote Parkinson, British historian and author

Industry is full of examples of how complexity has impacted organizations. One of the most devastating effects is that the workload goes up dramatically, but the results do not improve (or they actually get worse). Productivity is often adversely affected because there are too many different things that need to be done; thus, focusing on the right priorities is difficult. The work force becomes cynical or doubtful of management's direction and leadership, which is not suprising considering that they are working harder, only to find themselves falling further behind.

Complexity also adds more interactions between organizational units. These interactions, combined with the workload, lead to organizational stress, discontent, and errors. The people blame each other, or management, or the anonymous "they," which could be anyone from clients to peers to the executive team. This frustration is soon transmitted to customers, suppliers, and others with whom the organization interacts. A common attempt at fixing the problem is not to remove the complexity or stop its causes, but to reorganize, restructure, or rearrange the way work is done, and the people doing it.

Since no one is attacking the root cause of the problem (and thus not reducing the work that must be done), this doesn't help. In fact, it usually makes things worse, because now the status quo has been disrupted, and even the work that was going well is potentially impacted. One organizational-structure solution *does* have potential merit, if/when the complexity is dealt with, so let's consider it.

The Matrix Organization

When companies are started, there are usually only a few people involved. Someone has an idea and creates a product or service. He or she enlists the help of a cadre of associates to build a small organization. The initial group may include someone doing what we now call sales and marketing, another person doing production and procurement, and yet another doing finance, accounting, and administration. Think in terms of someone to create and sell "it," another person to make or buy "it," and a third person to keep the books, records, etc. It's a simple structure—at the start, that is.

Then the number of "it" grows in volume and variety, and the number of customers and suppliers grows, too. More people are added because the initial three people simply can't keep up with the workload. As the business grows, over the years, it becomes larger and larger, adding layers of people and layers of complexity. At some point, the idea emerges that the organization should be split into decentralized units that are focused on market segments.

This is a good idea that adds accountability and relevance. But it can also trap resources in the decentralized units and alter other organizational dynamics. Dedicated professionals in fields like engineering, purchasing, planning, and so on are now aligned with the needs of their business unit and its customers—which is good. Since there are only a few people with expertise in their discipline located within that unit, they are separated from their professional peers who reside in some functional silo at headquarters. This can inhibit the professional development of these decentralized specialists, and ultimately reduce their effectiveness within their units.

On the other hand, if they are retained in a functional structure (silo), their connection to the customers and the needs and goals of the profit-producing business unit are limited. What is the solution to such a complexity conundrum? Aha! Enter the matrix organization. The professional now has two bosses. One is in the business unit where he or she is located. The other is in the functional structure that is his or her home discipline. Simple, right? No. It's complex serving two masters whose goals may not coincide and whose expectations can be widely different. Time demands and conflicting priorities will build and are tough to resolve.

Shared Services and Functional Duplication

The increase of matrix organizations has created a number of complexities. To deal with the simplest ones—common shared services—companies have created centralized departments with that name. These are usually centralized at a corporate or regional headquarters. The functions centralized into shared services are usually information technology, human resources, accounting, finance, and legal and administrative work. Companies certainly don't need numerous decentralized and duplicated legal, accounting, information technology, or human resource functions. The centralized sharing of these types of services is far more efficient, uses smaller staffs, and works with one or two representatives in local offices as touch-points or coordinators. However, centralized shared-services people don't feel the pulse of the organizational business unit that is customer and competitor focused. Thus, companies invariably circle back to specialized support staff for the business unit.

Imagine the relationship complexity this matrix organization structure creates. Also recall that structure comes first but then leads to processes, culture, and relationships. Companies that neither had such complexity nor needed it suddenly create a new, more complex organizational structure when they decide to expand (proliferate) the products, customers, markets, business units, and countries served. But no one thinks of these future complications when the excitement about new products, new customers, and new sales revenues are at the forefront. It is only later, when tangled webs of complexity disrupt communications, bureaucratize administration, and confuse external contacts that the questions—and costs—pile up and the problems become apparent.

The Problem: Complexity in Duplication of Efforts

As supplier companies grow and multiple divisions sell to the same large customer, some strange occurrences start to pop up. The customers might see five or six sales representatives of the same company, each representing different business units, sitting in the waiting area on the same day. What does the customer think? It might think that the company employing all of those people sitting in their lobby is inefficient, disorganized, and probably doesn't know who's doing what. But it does; it just hasn't yet figured out how else to call on the customer. This is a symptom of complexity at work, and it reveals the lack of success in the struggle to manage it.

This problem was first addressed by some of the biggest and best companies, such as Procter and Gamble, Johnson and Johnson, and others. Clearly, each division, brand, or business unit wanted its products to be presented in the best possible way, with strong personal relationships and an effective support system. What, then, were they to do? The answer, used by not only P&G but also by many others, was to form selling teams that share support services and office facilities, and locate them close to the customer.

Selling Teams à la P&G and Wal-Mart's Model

The best-known example of this approach is Wal-Mart. Wal-Mart's headquarters was situated in an out-of-the-way, hard-to-reach, small town—Bentonville, Arkansas. In the early stages of Wal-Mart's growth, traveling there was difficult and time consuming. As Wal-Mart has grown, the number of selling teams and supplier offices located near its headquarters in Bentonville, Arkansas, has exploded. These supplier offices are intended to increase coordination and decrease the confusing impact of complexity. They do, when done correctly. Thus far, this approach is the best-known solution to this common form of organizational complexity. Surrounding Wal-Mart's offices are literally hundreds of "satellites" consisting of the many customer teams that represent its numerous suppliers, most located in Bentonville, AR.

But what about the dozens or hundreds of customers who are too small to benefit from the localized team approach? How do they cope with the multiple sales representatives from the same supplier, all sitting in the same waiting room? The same challenge faces sellers and buyers in many industries. Where the sellers are able to effectively use the selling-team concept, they do. When they cannot, they often resort to the approach used before the emergence of so many megacustomers. They use sales representatives that cover specific geographic or customer/market segments.

It is not possible to go back to the simple single-unit organizations from which the larger company grew. A solution remains that evolved as industries grew. Independent sales-representative firms used to be very common. These rep firms represented and sold multiple product lines and traveled in a given geographic or market territory (segment). In doing this, they were essentially the precursors of the localized company-staffed selling teams.

As Wal-Mart grew, it banished the sales reps, opting to deal directly with its suppliers. Wal-Mart didn't want to deal with any intermediaries; it wanted to deal directly with its suppliers. There are arguments as to whether this was to save the commission paid to the reps or to prevent the reps from carrying information on what Wal-Mart was doing to their other accounts, who were Wal-Mart's competitors. But those reasons matter little in the containment of complexity—the key is to simplify and reduce redundant and wasted time and people.

Sometimes, to Go Forward, You Must Go Back (to an Old Solution)

Many other companies did not follow Wal-Mart's practice and opted to allow independent sales reps to call on them. The companies/industries that continued to permit independent sales reps found them to be a good solution to their needs. Instead of having five or six salespeople in the lobby, a single sales rep (either an independent commission-based rep or multidivisional company employee) could handle all of the product lines and make the sales call on one or more of that customer's buyers. The more sophisticated sales-rep firms built an infrastructure not that different from the localized company sales teams, with showrooms, computerized order-tracking systems, and so forth.

In doing so, independent reps successfully performed major parts of those functions of a selling team. If these rep firms had strong strategic partnerships with the companies whose products they represented, this was, and in many cases still is, a viable alternative to creating another layer of organizational complexity. Situations like this must each be analyzed individually, and may not yield to cookie-cutter solutions. The key in managing complexity is to understand the needs of the customer (and the supplier) and construct the least-complex solution from the range of available options.

Complexity Impacts Mergers and Acquisitions, Too

The justification of many mergers is that there will be economic synergies created by combining functional units of the merger partners. Sometimes, trying to capitalize on such synergies creates new problems and complexity costs. This is an area in which complexity contributes to the failure of mergers to create any new economic value for the investors. Studies have proven that most mergers do not yield long-term economic value for the companies involved. There is a short-term benefit as redundancies are eliminated, and then the issue of complexity rears its ugly head. What seemed to be a simple combination of the two companies is not so simple after all. The preceding discussion about organizational complexity in selling situations is repeated in many other parts of the newly merged company. One of the reasons is likely that the complexity added by combining two sets of formerly competitive "DNA" embodied in cultures, structures, and processes of the merged companies leads to "turf battles," "fiefdoms," and more complexity, not less. And by now, we know that complexity is the enemy of profitability.

Study How Industry Leaders Have Managed Complexity

The tentacles of the Complexity Crisis spread far and wide. Like a fast-growing vine, they become entangled quickly and are difficult to untangle. There is much to be learned by looking at how leaders in different industries have adapted to the complexity issues created by size, growth, and expansion. This does not mean that industry leaders like Procter and Gamble, Johnson and Johnson, GE, and others have eliminated complexity. They have not. They have just worked at finding solutions longer and found some solutions that work for them. Complexity is still alive and well—and creating problems—even in the best of companies. (Remember Motorola and Dell cited earlier?)

The solutions to complexity will be different for each situation. The best solution, above all, is to recognize and contain complexity before it grows and spreads. Carefully consider the structures, processes, cultures, and relationships best suited to manage the causes of complexity. If this is done correctly, complexity's problems can be turned into competitive advantages.

How Unions Add Complexity

Labor Unions came into being in the first half of the twentiety century to do collective bargaining for employees, and to protect them against inconsiderate or downright brutal treatment by employers of that era. Bolstered by the Taft-Hartley Act and other labor laws, unions provided the employees with leverage against employers via the ability to strike and thus withhold work effort, and in negotiating pay, benefits, and working conditions.

At the time, unions served a valid function. As time passed, enlightened companies changed how they dealt with employees, either reducing the need for unions or at least rendering them far less important (and less powerful). Union membership dropped and, today, many believe that unions do at least as much harm as good for employees, since the terms of the union contract often undermine the employer's competitive position. At the very least, the presence of a union contract with employees adds complexity, which is the enemy of profitability.

Running a unionized operation is significantly more complex than running a nonunion one. Why is the union organizational setting so much more complex? Since unionism's growth goes back to management observing the right operating principles, behaviors, work rules, disciplinary practice, wage and hour rules, etc., the result was that all of these were written into a union contract, but in restrictive language.

To take just one example, consider the creation of too many job classifications. The purpose of job classifications was to protect workers' job rights by preventing management misbehavior like favoritism, nepotism, and a bunch of other -isms. All those job classes in a typical union shop require a process called "bumping and slotting" whenever increases or decreases in the work force occurred. This process usually recognized seniority (length of service) as the sole criteria for rights to the jobs that people wanted. Why? Because that takes away subjective decision factors like skill, ability, and experience. It also reduces favoritism, bias, and unfair practices. The issue is how the union contract is written. If it contains page after page of work rules, slotting, bumping, job assignment, incentive pay, and job classifications, then complexity rules. When a 2,000-employee plant has just 20 too many people—and mind you, with only 2 percent absenteeism, it takes about 40 extra people just to cover for absenteeism—*if* it decides to layoff 20 extra people to save $10,000 per week in wages, then as many as 500 people might change jobs over the next two to three weeks due to waves of bumping and slotting. This has a terrible effect on productivity and quality as people refamiliarized themselves to jobs they might have done months or even years ago, not to mention the administrative impact of tracking 500 job/people changes over a three-week period.

Vacation pay can be another problem, especially if it is a complex mixture of hourly base rate and actual incentive-earned rate. Another complexity is in determining who qualifies for holiday pay based on the schedule worked on the day(s) before and after the holiday. These are just a few examples of how unions cause complexity. Only with great union-management relations and careful attention to the consequences of contract provisions can this kind of complexity be kept in check.

19

NEW METHODS OF COSTING

When Old Measures Are Inadequate,
Create New Ones

*"Do not go where the path may lead, go instead
where there is no path and leave a trail."*
—Ralph Waldo Emerson

Linking Costs to the Causes

The practice of accounting made great progress in the latter part of the twentieth century when it introduced "activity-based accounting," which provides considerably better insight into how accounting and managerial behavior are interrelated. Since that time, however, the accounting profession has been taking a "policeman" approach, thanks to the misadventures of Enron, Global Crossing, WorldCom, and others. Being compliant with Sarbanes-Oxley is important, but it no more guarantees success than having an ISO-9000 compliance.

COMPLIANCE WITH REGULATIONS
AND CERTIFICATIONS DOES NOT
GUARANTEE SUCCESS

Sarbanes-Oxley is the new law passed in 2001, after the widely publicized accounting scandals involving misstatement of earnings. This law requires many new corporate safeguards against financial and accounting fraud/misstatements, including the requirement that a corporare CEO and CFO both sign to certify that financial statements are accurate under risk of criminal penalties. Many additional FASB (Federal Accounting Standards Board) rulings have also been issued in the past few years to support Sarbanes-Oxley.

ISO-9000 is one of a family of International Standards Organization certifications that confirm if a company complies with certain requirements. This particular one deals with documentation of the processes and operations, but has no safeguards that monitor whether the processes documented are good processes. Flawed processes can be superbly documented and the company can be ISO-9000 certified that it does things "perfectly"—even if they are the "perfectly wrong things to do."

Both simply say that you certify that what you did was done the way you said you'd do it (or in accordance with some standards that apply). Neither says that what was done was done the best way, or even a particularly good way. The blizzard of new accounting and governance regulations, FASB (Federal Accounting Standards Board) standards, etc. continues to focus on the reporting of gains, losses, and asset values. While these regulations add layer after layer of complexity, little attention has been devoted to improving core areas of management through better accounting analysis and reporting.

"God Is in the Details"

As famous architect Mies Van der Rohe said, "God is in the details." How and where does modern accounting help you better manage those details, especially when they involve the tension between innovation and complexity? How do you know how far to push innovation versus controlling complexity? The only way to know that answer is to understand what complexity costs, where to find its impact, and what effect it has on quality, service, profit, and growth. To accomplish this, you must measure some things that have not been measured. Fortunately, most of the raw data needed is already available somewhere in those corporate computer systems we all know and love—and rely on. The challenge is knowing what to look for in those corporate computer systems. There are four formulas that show the balance of factors that go into the "knowing."

TAC #8: FOUR FORMULAS FOR SUCCESS

1. Data + Organization = Information

2. Information + Insight = Knowledge

3. Knowledge + Experience = Wisdom

4. Wisdom + Imagination = Genius

As you can see, these formulas reveal a progression from data to information, to wisdom, and finally to genius. At each step, human intervention plays a key role. However, the very first equation is one where some new metrics derived from existing data must be employed. Only then can the human intervention begin to yield progress.

A very important warning is also in order. Mark Twain stated it very well. "It ain't what you don't know that gets you into trouble. It's what you know for sure that ain't so." Far too many decisions on such delicate matters as innovation versus complexity are being made on flawed understanding or prevailing wisdom and employ information that is either misunderstood or outright wrong.

As we go into this next section, I'll try to offer some examples of how to get better information, create better metrics, and therefore make better decisions—or at least decisions based on sound information and not misinformation.

New Accounting Metrics—Assigning Costs in New Ways

The accounting profession needs to catch up with the maelstrom of global business circa the twenty-first century. There must be new categories of entries and new descriptors that apply to the assignment of costs caused by, among other things, complexity. Variance accounts categorize the entries by the old terms of labor, overhead, and materials, but there is little or no segregation as to root causes. Just as standard cost accounting ignored activities, which necessitated the development of activity-based accounting, there must be a new set of entries that capture and assign the costs of complexity where they belong. To start any such process of change, it is useful to identify the likely causes and the places to look.

A PARTIAL LIST OF COMPLEXITY SOURCES—TO MEASURE AND ASSIGN COSTS

- **Transactions:** orders, invoices, payments, voucher entries, adjustments
- **Customers:** sales calls, unique products/programs/promotions, record keeping/reporting

- **Suppliers:** sales calls, unique components/materials/deals, record keeping/reporting, variability, and six sigma
- **Competition:** market segments, products, regions, countries, and distribution types
- **Obsolescence:** raw material, components, finished products, marketing/merchandising materials, closeouts, markdowns, scrap, administration
- **Forecasting:** variety, similarity/shifting, seasonality, geography, Bills of Materials, planning changes, schedule changes
- **Shipment:** destinations, routings, shipping instructions, manifests/paperwork, confusingly similar numbers/models/packages, DC locations
- **Staffing Costs, Learning Curve, and Training Costs**
- **Information Systems:** Electronic-data-interchange protocols, size of database, number of programs, memory, processing, documentation, network management, security
- **Currency Risks:** number of countries buying, selling, doing business, employees
- **Tax Returns:** number of states and countries, different tax codes, regulations
- **Incorporation and Officer Designations:** number of states and countries, governing law
- **Regulations:** number of states and countries, local codes, industry-related
- **Intellectual Property:** number of states and countries, patents, trademarks, copyrights

An exhaustive analysis of how to assign costs to complexity depends on a deep understanding of the business, its purpose, structure, processes, and culture/relationships. To get started, there are approaches that are applicable to a wide range of situations.

Measuring the staffing and support costs associated with a function or activity and then dividing by the number of transactions, events, or entities is a good way to start. This kind of measure will yield $ per transaction information like $ per purchase order, $ per customer order entered or shipped, or $ per deduction/claim resolved. These are useful metrics to expose the cost of complexity.

The challenge is to partition and quantify all of the expenses associated with specific classes of complexity-driven costs. To do this requires an insightful analysis of how budgets are organized and where expenses are charged versus where work is done. While this generality sets the stage for the necessary metrics, let's take each category and comment on specifics about how to capture the costs of complexity.

Transactions: Orders, Invoices, Payments, Voucher Entries, and Adjustments

Most companies can identify the number of customer only orders received, how many invoices result from those orders, how many payments are made, and how many claims or adjustments are processed. In fact, those functions are usually relatively segregated into organizational units specialized for those tasks. The personnel budgets—payroll costs, benefits, and support cost—are the easiest to gather. When this is done, the first step of determining the cost of an order transaction from beginning to end is underway. Accumulate the annual department expenses for order entry and order management and divide by the number of orders processed in a year. Do the same thing for the department that processes invoices and applies the cash. If there are separate people assigned to handle claims, deductions, etc., repeat the process.

Once the discrete tasks have all been counted and the expenses associated with doing them have been identified, a series of cost per transaction figures can be calculated and saved separately. They can also be totaled, to yield an end-to-end cost of processing a customer order, including the payment for it. I purposely omitted the fulfillment of the order, since that is a separate, identifiable, and manageable process. Unless your company is different from most I have seen, it will be surprising how much it costs to process a complete order from beginning to end.

Note that I did not encourage you to allocate any "top management costs" to this process. Some are certainly incurred in the process, but this allocation can become arbitrary and contentious and is not usually where the largest costs are incurred. We'll deal with that issue separately.

You might have noted that the topic of benchmarking has not been addressed. That is because the awareness and use of these metrics is so scattered and sparse. As more companies read and adopt this advice, new comparative data will emerge, and professional organizations can develop benchmarks. Until then, my advice is to benchmark against your own metrics and strive for continuous improvement on those.

The outcome of this step will allow you to to know what it costs to process a customer order from end to end.

Customers: Sales Calls, Products/Programs/Promotions, Record Keeping/Reporting

Maintaining good customer contact takes time and effort. This is the part of the organization that gets the orders, calls on the customers, and keeps them actively involved in the business. Whereas in the last metric we divided by the number of transactions, in this one, we will divide by the number of customers.

A customer is the entity that buys something from the company—orders it and pays for it. Customers come in all sizes, large and small. Customers require different kinds of attention, too. Some want to be visited, while others just want to order and receive what was ordered. Once again, go to the departmental budgets for sales and gather the expenses that are incurred by sales (don't forget commissions, which may be accounted for in a different budget). Sales is usually a people-and travel-intensive budget area. Additional sales costs are often found in samples to customers, premium freight, special customer-based trade show costs, and so forth. Find all of these expenses and total them. Don't worry that some customers cause you to incur more of these expenses than others—that is the next step. First, find what an average customer costs you to keep around.

Bear in mind a key point: averages are great for graphs and overall presentations, but they are deadly misleading for taking specific actions. You must identify where causes of the high-dollar items originate. Some customers are known to be high maintenance. Now it is time to identify who, why, and how much. That may or may not mean tracking every minute detail like copy costs and phone calls. It certainly means tracking the big-expense items. Most expense-budget details will show what the big expenses were, especially if the budget is sorted by descending annual expenses by department (or function).

The challenge is to identify which customers caused those big expenses to be incurred. That means a slightly different detail breakdown. In the previous transaction example, the breakdown was by the nature of the transaction. In this one, it is by the cause of the expense, identified by customer, or if it is a group of customers, by that segment of the business. Later, you will want to divide these costs by the sales revenue created by these customers to express them as a percent of sales. For now, you want to know which customers or groups of customers are costing you big bucks to serve. Don't forget to include in your expenses the cost of setting up a new customer in the computer system (that also may appear in a different budget).

Finally, sales should keep a call log, identifying who visited whom and when. This not only allows an analysis of whether sales time is being well spent, but it also provides a means to make sure that all customers get their fair share of attention and contact.

The outcome of this step will be to know what it costs to obtain, maintain, and serve a customer, both as an average and as a percent of sales to that customer.

Purchase Orders and Suppliers: Transactions, Sales Calls, Variability, and Six Sigma

This measurement combines elements of each of the prior two, with a few additional considerations. First, do the transaction analysis for purchase orders and payments just like the one for processing customer orders. Next, repeat the process of identifying what it costs to set up, buy from, and maintain a supplier, just as you did for a customer. If there is a certification process involved, don't forget to calculate the expenses for people and any travel needed to do that part as well.

If suppliers call on the buyers, this can become a very costly and wasteful process. Person-to-person interaction is important, but it can easily get out of control. If you calculate the same kind of information as you did in the sales example above, you can find the average cost of having a supplier

The same issues about high-maintenance customers apply to suppliers as well. Sort the expense budgets in descending-value order and look for large items—these are the tip-offs. Premium freight is usually one account that will stand out. It either means that your company doesn't allow enough lead-time (or makes too many last-minute delivery schedule changes) or that the supplier misses requested/promised delivery dates. When that happens, premium freight cost is incurred to deliver the materials in time for production/customer need and the supplier(s) should pay the premium freight costs. If they don't, the premium freight costs will show up as hidden costs—an unfavorable variance—in one of the variance accounts. Find it. Fix it. Eliminate the cause(s).

A meeting log for supplier visits to buyers (just like the sales call log) will be also useful and informative. You can review this to assure the right amount of time is spent with suppliers. Good relationships are important, but a sales call on a buyer can easily turn into "old buddies" wasting a disproportionate amount of a buyer's time. Beware of the lengthy business lunch, where the salesperson entertains the buyer, too. Sometimes this can be an attempt to gain favor in future purchases and sometimes it is just because they have become "old buddies." It is for this reason that many large companies rotate buyer assignments. Good relationships are valuable. "Too good" can be a source of a different form of complexity—a biased buyer making decisions for the wrong reasons.

A final area to watch cannot be tracked from financial statements. It is reciprocation in the form of "salespeople bearing gifts to buyers." This doesn't necessarily add to complexity per se, but it certainly adds to the risk of inappropriate buying decisions that favor a supplier and not the buyer's employer. Even the most inconsequential gifts can lead to feelings of obligation, which may (or may not) add to decision-making complexity, but at the very least it certainly adds to the risk of inappropriate decisions.

The outcome will be to know what it costs to place, receive, and pay for a purchase from end to end and how this occurs.

Control Complexity—Know Your Competition

Your complexity can increase greatly due to competitive pressures. The best way to control such outbreaks of complexity is to know your competition. Gathering competitive intelligence is a specialty, but it is one that can be learned and used to great advantage.

Different market segments, products, regions, countries, and distribution types all constitute places where competitive intelligence might be found. There is a wealth of information easily available. Use industry associations (if there is an association cost—dues, conventions, etc., this can be captured in expenses), or the government-published data on markets, industries, imports, exports, employment, and more. Someone must have the job of accumulating and tracking competitive intelligence, and that person's cost and support costs can be tracked as complexity-related costs too. Use the Internet to create a company Web site section devoted to competitive intelligence, and limit access to those who need to know what is posted there. This is a cost-effective solution, but it is not free. Capture that cost and add it to your "Competitive Intelligence Costs." The use of competitive intelligence can be very valuable—but you do need to be aware of what it cost to gather it. It is usually a complexity-avoidance cost, rather than a hidden-problem cost.

Who Sells, Who Buys, How Much?

In this regard, I encourage you to organize your market knowledge in this manner. I call it a "who sells, who buys" matrix. (Spreadsheet programs like Microsoft Excel work well for this.)

Who Buys–Who Sells Matrix

Market: Bikes to U.S. Retail

Suppliers	Customers	Wal-Mart	Cust mix %	Target	Cust mix %	Toys"R"Us	Cust mix %
			A				
Pacific		3.6	54%	0.6	9%	0.8	12%
B	Supplier Share	57%		30%		28%	
Huffy		1.5	31%	0.5	10%	0.9	18%
	Supplier Share	24%		25%		31%	
Magna		0.4	19%	0.6	29%	0.5	24%
	Supplier Share	6%		30%		17%	
Misc.		0.3	17%	0.2	11%	0.2	11%
	Supplier Share	5%		10%		7%	
All other		0.5	13%	0.1	3%	.05	13%
	Supplier Share	8%		5%			
Total Cust. Sales		6.3		2.0		2.9	
		100%		100%		100%	

How to read this matrix:

A = Wal-Mart buys 54 percent of its total bike purchases from Pacific, 31 percent from Huffy, etc.
B = Pacific sells 57 percent of its total bike sales to Wal-Mart, 30 percent to Target, etc.

Note: All information is for example only—it is not actual data. This matrix was done with unit sales. By assuming an average selling price/unit, it can be converted to a $ sales matrix.

Kmart/ Sears	Cust mix %	Sport. Goods	Cust mix %	Other Mass.	Cust. Share	Total Units	Total %
0.3	4%	0.4	6%	1.0	15%	6.7	100%
20%		29%		19%			
0.6	12%	0.3	6%	1.1	22%	4.9	100%
40%		21%		21%			
0.2	10%	0.2	10%	0.2	10%	2.1	100%
13%		14%		4%			
0.1	6%	0.3	17%	0.7	39%	1.8	100%
7%		21%		13%			
0.3	8%	0.2	5%	2.2	58%	3.8	100%
20%		14%		42%			
1.5		1.4		5.2		19.3	
100%		100%		100%			

Down one side, list the top 10–20 +/- competitors. Across the top, list the top 10–20 +/- customers. Allow two lines and two columns for each. Then at the intersection, post the sales of each competitor, to each customer, and use the spreadsheet to calculate the percent of the total each represents both vertically and horizontally. Finally, add an "Other" row and column. If you have hard data for a customer or competitor, make the "Other" column one that calculates the difference between that total (the hard number) and the sum of your "estimated" numbers. This will tell you if you know where customers buy or competitors sell, and how much of a gap there is in your knowledge (data). If you don't have confidence in the "Total" numbers, let the computer add the rows and columns and decide later whether to plug an estimated number in the "All Other" or the Total column.

What? You say that's a hard matrix to complete? Of course it is. Most people claim that they know all about their competitors and their customers; however, very few can complete this valuable matrix. Once you have done it, each successive time will get easier, as those involved are sensitized to what information they didn't know and will pick up on competitive intelligence to help complete the matrix more accurately. This is an essential tool if you are to decide on strategy and tactics—which customers and what business to go after—and why, how, and where complexity figures into the decision.

This matrix approach can also be used in the analysis of purchasing opportunities and vendor importance. It is especially useful in coordinating buys among units of large, multidivisional companies. One other factor to consider is that this matrix illustrates both opportunities and vulnerabilities (the concentration of sales or purchases). At the same time you are doing this analysis, it is likely your competitors are too!

This outcome will be to record what you know (and don't know) about your customers, competitors and suppliers.

Obsolescence—Inventory and More

Obsolescence, especially inventory obsolescence combined with excess or noncurrent inventory, is the evidence of forecast errors, buying errors, execution errors, and most of all, of complexity. This is one of the most obvious costs of complexity.

Inventory obsolescence manifests itself in many forms: raw material, components, work-in-process, semifinished products, and finished products. Unfortunately, only finished products can be sold, albeit at a distressed price. Occasionally, the purchasing function can dispose of/return standard components or materials, but again, usually at a cost. There is also obsolescence in noninventory items: marketing/merchandising materials, catalogs, price sheets, photos, displays, etc. The use of the Web and digital imaging has reduced, but certainly not eliminated, these collateral material costs of obsolescence. In extreme cases, obsolescence can also affect tooling, equipment, even entire plants/offices, and the people who run them and work in them.

An important analysis is to see if a large proportion of obsolescence is attributable to specific customers or product lines, distribution channels, etc. If such costs are simply bundled into expense accounts and spread uniformly across all classes of customers, suppliers, products, etc., then the less-costly (to serve) customers are subsidizing the more costly ones. This can create risks of losing the better customers because they are, in essence, being overcharged.

There are also bad customers. In most companies (according to work done by Larry Selden and Geoffrey Colvin for their book *Angel Customers and Demon Customers*), there is a group of customers (20 percent of them) that account for most of the profit and value created and a comparable group (20 percent of them) that actually destroy value, causing losses. This latter group must be addressed, since it is likely that they are contributors of costly complexity in the business. These are mostly bad customers until or unless they are reformed or retrained to do business differently

The outcome of this will be to know about some of the most important effects of complexity and where the money has gone.

Forecasts Will Always Be Wrong

Forecasts are predictions about the future and, as such, are destined to be wrong. The more volatile the markets are, and the more demand there is, the greater the forecast errors that usually result. The less familiar the company and its people are with the markets and products, the more likely it is that forecasts will be wrong. The more complexity in the business, the more likely, the forecasts will be wrong. In addition, the less familiar the areas are where complexity has grown, the less accurate those forecasts will be.

If the business has seasonality, weather dependency, and similar difficult-to-predict patterns, more complexity will drive a painful array of costs resulting from forecast errors. Repacking, scrap, rework, mix changes, schedule changes, excessive setups, premium freight, etc. are all symptoms of forecast errors, whose root cause, in many cases, is the addition of complexity. Accumulate these costs. Use a matrix if you wish to list the cause categories down one side and the expense accounts impacted across the top, dropping the numbers in at the appropriate intersection. It is imperative that complexity costs be captured and assigned to the responsible areas, such that the economic impact of adding complexity is quantified and assigned to the likely causes. Only then can future decisions be guided by the right kind of information.

The outcome of this section will be to know which forecasts are likely to be wrong more than others.

More Places, More Customers, More Suppliers Equal More Mistakes

More interactions and more transactions involving more locations inevitably lead to more opportunities for error, and more administrative costs. To begin developing new metrics in this area, it is important to analyze past experience and use that knowledge to decide what to measure and how. Capture the costs of errors and define the root causes, the class of trade, customers, suppliers, products, and so forth. Analyze errors by the destinations, routes, and type of material, mode of transportation, shipping instructions needed, manifests/paperwork required, and so forth. Patterns of waste will emerge. Costs will be exposed that can be assigned back to where they originated. Watch for simple causes like confusing similarity in product numbers, distribution centers, locations, models, and package configurations. Add helpful visual cues like color codes, icons, etc. to avoid such errors.

Once errors have occurred, the cost of those errors must be captured and traced back to the root causes, some of which will be complexity related, and others will be systemic, operational, or execution errors. The key point in this case is to quantify what can reasonably be quantified, and understand what caused those costs—and what to do about it—and especially how to factor this knowledge into future decisions. A final point in this area: the best way to reduce errors caused by complexity is to reduce complexity.

The outcome of this part is that you will know and see how proliferation adds complexity.

Staffing, Learning Curve, and Training Costs

Complexity drives up the number of people and the cost of systems needed to track, manage, and control the new, more complex enterprise. Thus far, this chapter has focused on how to accurately assess costs of each kind of complexity. Let's now focus on a different metric related to complexity. What you will normally find in any organization that has been crippled by complexity is an increase in the head count, either in regular employees or those artificial stopgaps—temporaries or contract workers. It is important to get to the bottom of what is really happening, thus the term "full-time equivalents" (FTE) is useful. Express the staffing level of each meaningful division of the business in FTEs and track the trend over the past two to three years. Then track a different set of metrics. Divide the sales revenue and the profit revenue by the headcount to come up with sales per head count and profit per head count. Choose an appropriate measure of profits. I suggest earnings before interest and taxes (EBIT) because it is a commonly used measure of profits. If you plot this data for the past two or three years back, and do it on a trailing twelve-months (TTM) graph, the trend line will emerge.

THE TRAILING TWELVE-MONTH
GRAPH (TTM)

A TTM graph takes twelve months of data, averages it, and plots the value. Then for succeeding months, add a new month's data to the twelve, drop the oldest month's data, and average it again, and then plot that value. This kind of graph is a useful tool for many measures, so remember this TTM description. It is particularly useful because the resulting line shows a trend (over the past twelve months, to be exact) which reveals the direction of the metric graphed. The monthly data can be plotted on the same graph, with the TTM line superimposed on it. This shows both month-to-month variation and longer-term trend directions. By using the current year's budget data, a target point can be plotted on the vertical axis at the end of the year, which shows where the TTM line will end if budgeted performance is attained. A quick look shows whether the TTM line (trend) is heading toward the objective (budget) or not.

Use a TTM graph to plot head count in FTEs by location, division, department, or whatever organizational unit makes sense. Do the same for metrics like sales per head count and profit per head count, and then consult the graphs at each month end to evaluate the trends. Since complexity almost invariably impacts the number of people needed to manage a given part of a business, these TTM charts on head count will reveal where this impact is greatest. Your job is then to discover why and what to do about that.

The outcome of this part is to know where your head count is going up and understand if that is appropriate, or driven by complexity.

Information Systems

Information-systems costs are among the most elusive in which to track the costs of complexity. Computers, using well-designed software, can process millions of transactions with lightning speed and transmit data around the globe in seconds. The operative phrase here is well-designed software. Information-systems management must be part of the decision process at the "use it or lose it" stage of fighting complexity, because the inherent design of the system is a powerful tool to use it, and a huge obstacle if not designed and used properly.

Size and configuration of databases, number of programs, memory, processing, documentation, network management, storage, security, and EDI protocols are all elements of a system that must be carefully considered during strategic planning. The computing hardware is another element. Although hardware costs are not usually the largest ones, they are most identifiable, since hardware resides in boxes and these boxes can be counted and valued. Valuing the complexity cost in information-systems terms usually translates into added cost on the input of data, the output of reports, and the amount of memory the system needs to store the necessary information. Transactions flow rapidly. At the boundaries, people must be involved, and that is where complexity costs extra. Measures of information systems costs are best done on a large (macro) basis, such as a percent of net sales for the division or enterprise, and then at a closer (micro) level, at each user location or data center. Add all the staff costs, facility costs, utility costs, and maintenance (hardware and software) costs and see how the percent of net sales for the individual user locations vary. The ones that are high are probably afflicted by complexity.

The outcome of this part is that you know where and how informationsystems costs are impacted by complexity.

Finance, Regulatory, Legal, and Human Resources

These topics are grouped because they are all more-readily measured on a location or business-unit basis than on transactions per se. Similar approaches to creating new measurements and tracking progress will likely work for all of these support service areas.

Finance—Currency Exchange Rates

The more countries in which a company does business leads to more currency-exchange-rate risks. This is a direct monetary impact, thus it is readily captured. What may not be so readily captured are the causes. If the impact of exchange rate is localized, a reasonable assumption is that complexity will impact the results regardless of the currency. But, the more places you do business, the more chances there are for currency fluctuations alone to cause unexpected economic impacts that were not planned, and in many cases these are largely uncontrollable. Currency hedging is one way to reduce currency risk. When done correctly, it is simply a form of insurance. When done incorrectly, it is tantamount to gambling on the outcome of multidimensional economic matters that affect exchange rates. Since these are geopolitical issues, exchange rates can be affected by both economics and politics.

The number of countries in which a company is doing business, hiring employees, and operating facilities adds immeasurably to its complexity. Some of this complexity is measurable, but the plethora of laws, rules, customs, regulations, political factors, and cultural norms that impact the company will far exceed the few metrics I can propose here. Start at the macro levels and apply the metrics described earlier: cost per transaction, sales and profit per head count, etc., and these will expose the high-cost countries and provide clues as to why they are high cost.

Finance—Taxes

Most countries collect taxes. This means more tax returns to file and tax codes to understand. The greater the number of states and countries, the higher the tax accounting costs. The increase in tax accounting costs are one measure to quantify the amount of complexity added due to the impact of filing and paying taxes. When companies are enthused about expanding in search of growth, details like creating legal entities, choosing/designating officers, and local rules and regulations get lost in the exuberant scramble to sell something to a new customer in a new place. But all of these are finite actions that have a cost associated with initiating and maintaining them. The greater the number of states and countries, the higher the cost to manage tax matters.

Finance—Banking

Banking and finance are now among the most global of industries, with trillions of dollars flowing around the world each day. Setting up banking and financial relationships in multiple locales doesn't cost that much money per se, but it does require managerial time and attention. And in business, time is money. Needing to know banking and financial regulations and requirements adds complexity for financial officers. Errors in this area can be avoided by using the right expertise and process, but those that slip through can be huge and costly.

Regulatory

Regulatory compliance is also a large complexity-related cost. The more-developed countries tend to have more of it, while less-developed countries tend to have more cultural or local-custom issues to understand and with which you will have to comply.

Legal—Intellectual Property (IP)

A characteristic of today's global business environment and rapid product life cycles is that products and services fall prey to knockoffs faster than ever before. This requires careful management of the few legal IP protections that exist for new and innovative products and services. Moreover, there is vastly uneven enforcement of IP protection in the various countries of the world. In some places, it follows an orderly rule of law, as it does in the United States. In many others, including some of the most popular sites for outsourcing (like China, Thailand, etc.), the rules of IP law are limited at best, irrelevant at worst. The laws often exist, but enforcement is often local in nature and can be greatly affected by illicit dealings among the parties and the courts. Further, as countries develop more IP laws, local "entrepreneurs" buy the protection rights to well-known global brands and sell them back to the foreign owners for a handsome profit. This happened to me in Spain twenty years ago, even before globalization was so pervasive. Before Huffy was doing much bicycle business in Europe, Spanish "entrepreneurs" bought the rights to many well-known U.S. brand names. I was only aware of two: Huffy and Nike, but I am sure there were many more. We paid dearly to regain the legal rights to our brand name.

The complexities of intellectual-property management are yet another example of how complexity problems arise unexpectedly. Counterfeit products, gray-market products diverted from legitimate channels, and other variations all add to competitive pressure. The speed with which many of these emerge is surprising. Since complexity in a company slows the company's processes, that company becomes even more susceptible to rapid knockoffs, illegal/counterfeit copies, and other illicit forms of competition that circumvent IP laws.

Human Resources

Employment at will is a common practice in the United States. If you have too many people, you fire some, or lay them off to be called back later. Such matters are not nearly so simple in many other countries. Most European countries have much more stringent (and employee-protective) rules about the employer's obligations if a job is to be eliminated. These usually involve payments to the displaced employees over an extended time period. Someone has to understand these laws both before and after a foreign office with employees is established. In some countries, the traditions are stronger than the laws. Japanese employers have a great social obligation to treat employees fairly if a job is to be eliminated. Without detailing specific situations further, remember that each of these areas add to the impact of complexity, which adds costs, restricts freedom, and can be very damaging to a company's operations and financial results. These costs, of course, are buried among many other unrelated ones in the overall administrative expenses of the company.

The outcome of these sections is that you know about and realize the many aspects of complexity with which you may be unfamiliar or at least not knowledgeable.

Conclusion

In this chapter, I have discussed at length how to create new measurements, but mostly using part of old measuring techniques applied in new ways to new forms of complexity. I encourage readers to invent their own new metrics. Benchmark against your own new metrics and drive continuous improvement, learning as you proceed. Use this to improve white-collar productivity and to support better budgeting/planning processes.

Do your homework—learn what is already available—so you don't have to create the added complexity of reinventing the wheel. The key point to take away is the importance of recognizing how and where complexity causes costs, and finding ways to quantify it—to assign the costs caused by the complexity to the root causes. Once these complexity costs are recognized, steps can be taken to identify and address root causes of the complexity. The goal is to reduce complexity, to control it, and keep it from recurring—or to use it for competitive advantage and price accordingly.

Remember, complexity is persistent. Even after it is driven out of a company or organization, vigilance is required to keep it from sneaking back in. Only if new and better metrics exist—call them early-warning indicators—can companies recognize its reappearance, and once again, drive it out and keep it out.

A Challenge to the Accounting Profession

When such a significant element of hidden costs goes unnoticed for so long, it probably indicates that there are gaps in the accounting system metrics. I hope *The Complexity Crisis* will serve as a challenge to the accounting profession to create appropriate metrics to categorize and manage this important drain on profit.

Decades ago, during the quality movement, quality organizations created a cost-of-quality metric, which is now widely used. Activity-based cost systems helped assign expenses to the appropriate cost areas and the activities that caused them. Nothing in the accounting system tracks the hidden costs of complexity as they accumulate in catchall accounts such as deductions, allowances, variances, reserves for obsolescence, and so forth. Nearly all of these can be assigned to causative factors. It is time for the accounting profession to turn its attention from helping the government police fraudulent reporting, and help companies achieve improved profitability and competitiveness through a more insightful measurement of complexity-driven costs.

THE BIG PICTURE

Tying It All Together

> *"In theory there is very little difference
> between theory and practice; in practice
> there is a lot of difference."*
> —John Mariotti

Too many business books cover every possible aspect of a topic except its context within the overall management of a business. This book covers how to recognize and deal with a particularly serious crisis. Therefore, this chapter must provide the overall business context needed to remedy this crisis caused by complexity, and integrate those concepts into the action plans to keep it from recurring. To do that, I will begin by outlining six major topics that either lead to complexity or are dramatically impacted by complexity—or both. I will also combine some of the key aspects of complexity (covered earlier in the book) with snippets of a couple of important concepts (from some of my prior books) that will help manage complexity and manage the business better, simultaneously.

I have included a brief section on what is arguably the most important element in both the management of complexity and the management of a company—leadership. Finally, I have devoted the last part of this chapter to a "framework for thought" that will help manage complexity without stifling innovation or the quest for growth. This is an ambitious task, but I believe it pulls together the understanding of the Complexity Crisis with the entirety of the business.

The Six Major Topics

There are six major topics that must be understood to compete and succeed in spite of complexity in this competitive global twenty-first-century business environment.

SIX MAJOR TOPICS

1. The Current Environment
2. The Curse of Complexity
3. Strategic Outsourcing—Boon or Bane?
4. The Value Network
5. Partnerships in an Era of Growing Complexity
6. Leadership—Creating a Path to the Future

The Current Environment

Never before has the world been so big and so small at one time. Some claim it is "flat," but that analogy may be an oversimplification. What better describes the global marketplace are two things:

1. Latent overcapacity—for almost everything
2. Global parity—caused by technology and market forces

Latent capacity means that given an opportunity to sell something, the production capacity for almost anything can be started up somewhere in the world in a surprisingly short time. Even if there is not an alternate competitive source now, there can be one, and very quickly. All it takes is a large market opportunity—or a large customer like Wal-Mart—to motivate a new producer to enter the market.

Global parity means that given a little time, companies around the globe can learn how to make almost anything (or provide almost any service). They can gain access to the technology, transmit the information anywhere in the world instantly, and thus erase many of the advantages of the incumbent competitors. There are only two advantages that are not vulnerable to the threats of "latent overcapacity" and "global parity," and these are having the best people and having relationships with the best partners.

Most major industries have proven that over time, the key competitors—those controlling the majority of the market—consolidate down to three or four. This leads to intense buying pressure and very little leverage for sellers. The trap of "Selling More for Less" (the title of one of my articles) is an insidious one. More units, more services, more software, and more hardware, all for fewer dollars, euros, yen, or whatever. Trends like this permeate the global markets of the twenty-first century and they are dramatically worsened by complexity. Not only must you sell more units for less, but you must also somehow overcome the higher (hidden) costs of complexity that drive up your total costs, right when you planned for and needed them to go down.

The Curse of Complexity

While capacity can spring up almost anywhere and faster than ever, demand is not so elastic. Demand exists where there is wealth, needs, wants, and purchasing power. This demand is a much harder beast to corral. Finding high-growth demand in a low-growth (developed) world is hard; sometimes it is impossible. There is great demand in the underdeveloped parts of the world, but little purchasing power to go with it. Thus it is a devilish choice: go after markets where the money is, but where intrinsic growth is low or zero, or go after huge potential markets where there is precious little money to pay for the goods, thus stifling growth a different way.

The solution for too many companies is to sell everything, everywhere, every way they can, and in doing so, these companies drown themselves in complexity. And there is no measurement system to warn them, or even to tell them it is happening. They learn after the fact. At the end of the accounting period, managers feel like they have arrived at the scene of a crime—right after it has been committed—and the money and the perpetrators are gone.

To make matters worse, more suppliers farther away means longer, more complex supply chains and more volatile demand in a hyper-competitive market—with less and less time to respond to changes. This adds up to trouble. Product life cycles are shrinking constantly, and that also means trouble. Add a healthy dose of too many of everything—commodities, products, customers, suppliers, markets, employees, subcontractors—and a business can become very troubled, very fast.

Strategic Outsourcing—Boon or Bane?

This is the most attractive lure since the sirens' call of Greek mythology. You can get it in China, subcontract it to India, import it from South America—but so can your competitors. Thus, where is the competitive advantage in that strategy? If you can buy (or rent) know-how, capacity, capability, etc., so can your competitors, and perhaps worse yet, so can your customers. There are times and circumstances when strategic outsourcing is a viable strategy. In fact, once the pros and cons, myths and mysteries of outsourcing are well understood, it can be a key part of an effective competitive strategy. But only if you fully understand the complexity of the entire value chain and how, where, and why your approach is a better one.

I recall hearing Geoffrey Moore (author of *Inside the Tornado* and other books) speak about the issue of deciding what to continue to do and what to outsource. He used the terms "core" and "context." Do what is core to your business, and outsource what is context.

Companies often err by giving away what is core during outsourcing. Be very careful in global outsourcing that you do not give away what is core to your business. Many have done so naively, with the best of intentions, and now rue the day. One of the most notable was Schwinn Bicycle Company, which gave away its core bicycle design and production know-how not once, but *twice*—first to Giant Bicycle of Taiwan and then again to China Bicycle Company (CBC) of Shenzhen, China. The result was that Giant came to the United States and took a large share of Schwinn's dealer market position. Then CBC finished off the job, essentially taking over the rest of Schwinn's position and relegating the once-proud company to a brand name in a stable of Chinese-made bicycle-product lines. The Schwinn brand is now sold at Wal-Mart, which once would have been anathema to a famous bicycle-dealer brand.

Also remember the famous words of philosopher John Ruskin (right off the Baskin-Robbins wall): "There is scarcely anything in the world that some man cannot make a little worse, and sell a little more cheaply. The person who buys on price alone is this man's lawful prey." Customers can create competitors with a few keystrokes on a computer or a global phone call. Take nothing for granted, and understand the complexity of the world in which you compete.

Some of the most tragic mistakes in outsourcing are the reasons behind it. Companies choose to move a problem to a faraway supplier in hopes that the supplier will fix the problem. Unfortunately, it may not be within the supplier's capability or interest to solve an inherited problem from a selfish customer. When you move an ugly problem further away from the source of its creation—and complexity is one of the ugliest—it doesn't make things better; it makes them worse. Fix the problems, then, if you still choose to, outsource the work.

Another misguided reason for adding complexity via outsourcing is to gain competitive advantage. What? A supplier who knows how to do something that creates competitive advantage will sell it to the highest bidder or perhaps to all who will pay for it. If you can rent or buy a competitive advantage, it won't be one for long, because others can rent or buy it, too. A veteran purchasing executive I worked with always told me when I asked for some special treatment or deal: "Be careful. If they'll do it *for* you, they'll probably do it *to* you, later on." This is especially true in countries where the rule of law is weak and the bonds of family are strong. The supplier may pledge not to sell around you to your competitor or customer, but his nearby brother-in-law will be glad to start a business to do just that.

The Value Network

The term "supply chain" is both a misnomer and an obsolete characterization of what it tries to describe. First, it is almost never a chain. The word *chain* conveys a linear set of links connected to one another in series. A chain is only as strong as its weakest link, so many companies are fortunate that their so-called supply chain is not really like a chain. The right term for the configuration is a network. As an exercise, simply diagram yours, from end to end (raw material to end user/consumer), and see what your supply chain looks like.

Next, realize that "supply" isn't the end goal, "value" is. Thus, since 1997 I have been referring to supply chains as "value networks." I described the Value Network briefly in a chapter of my book *Making Partnerships Work*. The Value Network is a series of nodes, joined by links, which is limited only by the cooperation of the people and the capability of information technology. It has a scope of global dimensions. People in the nodes (working as partners, hopefully) make decisions and take actions, from production to procurement to distribution, to logistics, etc. The links are the physical moves of material (or in service situations, the actual service delivery).

Virtually all companies have value networks that connect them with suppliers and customers. People using IT and logistics systems and tools operate the networks. Wherever and however the value network consistently creates and delivers the best value, you will find the global winners. Elsewhere, like a broken spider web, you will find the remains of the losers, hanging together, and hanging on by threads.

Partnerships in an Era of Growing Complexity

Earlier, I stated that people and partners are the key competitive differentiators—unless they are drowned in complexity. Find the best

211

people—those with talent, experience, expertise, skills, and imagination—and bring them together with strong leaders who will infuse them with passion. Then find the best partners to work with collaboratively. That is the formula for success in this era or any other. I said this in my first book, *The Power of Partnerships,* and I believe it more deeply than I did then, over a decade ago.

This interdependent partnership relationship seems to bridge the complexities and stand the test of time. This is not a partnership in the legal sense. It is one built upon trust, open information sharing, and communications with balanced risks and rewards that make it a good deal for all partners. Good partnerships are synergistic and added value is created for all partners. Those kind of partnerships usually last. If they are strong enough, they might even withstand the pressure of a huge customer who decides it wants to buy direct. When customers choose to become competitors, there are usually fundamental partnership problems both ways—with the customer and with the supplier—and if you are caught in the middle, it's a bad place to be.

Not all relationships are, or can become, partnerships. Only those built on trust have a chance. The four powerful partnership types in the value network can be easily recalled by the acronym CAST: Customers, Associates, Suppliers, and Truth-Tellers. If you make these choices wisely and build true partnerships, success is much more likely.

Leadership—Creating a Path to the Future

Last, but certainly most important of the six, is the imperative for strong leadership. Even with the strongest of partners, the right leadership is critical to success. Leadership is often confused with management—the two are both important, but quite different.

I was involved in an executive leadership conference some years ago, where I asked Robert Galvin, Sr., retired CEO of Motorola, if leadership could be taught. His answer was, "Not exactly, but it can be modeled for others to observe and learn." Pursuing the topic of leadership further, I asked him what leaders really do. I have never forgotten his answer. "Leaders," Galvin said, "take people to places they've never been before and are afraid to go alone." In the years that followed, as I thought about his statement, I added this phrase: "And they go along with them." To clarify the difference between managers and leaders, Galvin's example also works well. When a trip is being considered, managers make sure the trip plans are done, the route is clear, and the arrangements are in order. Leaders engage the people to go on the trip.

While that short example is a good description, in an era of growing complexity, it falls short of stating what a leader's role must be. There are two parts to the answer—the leader's role and the leader's responsibilities. The role has three parts:

- To create a clear understanding of, and healthy dissatisfaction with, the current reality
- To build a shared vision of a new, better reality as a goal
- To create an environment in which people are motivated to move from former to latter

There are four key responsibilities of a leader in this role:

- To provide and/or assure that the necessary resources are available
- To clear obstacles, maintain progress, develop metrics to measure progress, and stay on track

- To go along on the journey
- To celebrate wins, mourn losses, and never give up striving for the shared vision of the goal

When complexity afflicts an organization, it is easy for people to lose their bearings and lose their way. A leader will keep them on track and focused on the end goal. To manage that complexity, a leader's toughest decisions involve setting priorities. It is here that strong leaders must have three characteristics:

1. Courage—to make the tough decisions
2. Character—to be worthy of the organization's respect
3. Competence—to know the right things to do and when to do them

If the leader is deficient in any of those three, the pressures of unprecedented complexity will bring him or her down.

Once those three are in place, that leader must then do three more things so his/her organization will be successful in the face of adversity and complexity. The leader must help the people:

1. Find meaning in what they are doing
2. Find the points that provide the most leverage
3. Above all, create a sense of purpose among the people

A leader who does this with *passion* will be ready to face complexity and turn it to the advantage of his/her organization. Start as you would any journey. Figure out where you are now. Then chart a path to where you want to be.

Growth—the Elusive Goal

Ask a variety of executives to tell you how fast their markets are growing and you'll get a variety of answers. First, there will be some waffling about what exactly their target markets are. Trying to aim at a vaguely defined, dimly seen target is difficult enough, but hitting a target that is not well defined is nigh impossible. But let's assume the best case—they can state their target market definitions and begin to answer the question about growth. There will be a lot of imprecise words like "about," "approximately," and "sort of," followed by an answer that spans a range of numbers. Why? Because defining market growth rates is a challenging task in such a dynamic, global business world.

If the executive(s) can answer with a narrow range (say, 3 to 4 percent per year), the next question is to ask what growth they are planning for their businesses. The answer will invariably be a higher number than the market growth. Why? Because that is what investors and/or Wall Street expect of them. "Beat the market." But how can they do that?

In an earlier chapter, I stated that there were only five ways to grow:

1. Take share from existing competitors.
2. Expand the market with innovative new offerings; capture a larger share of that expansion.
3. Shift the mix to higher price/value products.
4. Enter new markets (still subject to numbers 1–3 of this list—there will be entrenched competitors).
5. Create an entirely new market.

These presuppose that the core competencies and capabilities that got the company to its current position are transferable to those desired new market positions. And most companies will make that assumption without pausing to assess its accuracy. Then they will attack on all fronts at once, in hopes that one or more of the attacks will work. The result of this drive for growth is—you guessed it—rampant complexity. Since there are no current measures for complexity and its impact on the business, the first wake-up call will be when the top line goes up and the bottom line goes down.

Runaway Proliferation of Everything

If complexity is born of the runaway proliferation of everything in search of high growth in low-growth markets, why does management do it? They do it with the best of intentions, reaching for goals that are set too high, or without understanding the consequences of their actions until afterward. Just think about the excitement when there is a major new product or new market initiative undertaken to gain sales and (hopefully) profit growth. That excitement often blinds management to the obstacles and complexity that lie ahead.

Globalization just makes this growth-driven complexity problem worse, especially if American companies do not understand the cultural differences of the markets in which they're trying to compete. My friend John Anderson, an international consultant, always told me, "Selling and doing business abroad is about 80 percent the same as in the United States, but you'd better know what/where the 20 percent differences are or they'll kill you." Creating legal business entities abroad is a complex and costly endeavor. Protecting intellectual property rights abroad—if there is enough law enforcement to do so—is equally costly and complex. Dealing with social and labor customs is different, and that leads to many other issues. Just imagine the initial challenges that add to complexity: language, currency, regulations, politics, culture, tax, import/export, customs, logistics, and many more.

The Complexity Factor™ Metric

To develop a single metric that can adequately present all of the aspects of complexity is not realistic. On the other hand, within similar kinds of businesses, just as six sigma became a relatively universal quality metric, there is value in a large, macro type of indicator. The following calculation is not so sensitive that being off by a few part numbers, a few suppliers, a few customers, etc. will render it unusable. What is important is to see how dramatically the index fluctuates when certain parts of it are changed in a quantum manner.

The best approach to using the CF is to compute your own and then try to drive it lower and lower; essentially, benchmark against yourself. In most cases, a comparison of two similar competing companies serving the same industry will find the one with the lower Complexity Factor will be the more profitable of the two. But there are many other factors that the CF doesn't consider, such as the degree of vertical integration, the amount of outsourcing employed, etc., so comparisons from company to company can be misleading. A comparison within your own company from month to month and year to year will show if you are gaining or losing ground to complexity.

Different kinds of industries have different criteria as to what constitute a product, a location, and so forth. These parts of the equation will have to be developed on an industry-by-industry basis. For example, a product SKU in a bank will differ from one in a hotel or an accounting-services company, but as long as there is a consistency within the company, the Complexity Factor will provide a valuable benchmarking tool to monitor the company's relative complexity.

THE COMPLEXITY FACTOR™ (CF) CALCULATION

To calculate the Complexity Factor™ (CF) requires six mathematical steps.

1. Add together the number of employees (FTEs), the number of customers (active and inactive), and the number of suppliers (all, not just inventory items).

2. Multiply this sum times the number of finished-product SKUs (active and inactive, but still on the books).

3. Multiply the result times the number of markets (kinds of markets-consumer, industrial, OEM, etc.).

4. Multiply this result times the number of meaningful locations (not counting small, remote sales offices, etc.).

5. Multiply the outcome times the number of countries in which the company has a legal entity (division, subsidiary, plant, etc.).

6. Finally, divide by annual sales revenue.

As an equation:

$$CF = \frac{(\#Suppliers + \#Customers + \#Employees)*SKUs*Markets*Locations*Countries}{Sales\ Revenue}$$

The result will be a number. The smaller the number, the less complex the company, and most likely, the more profitable the company will be compared to others in its competitive arena.

A few simpler measures are also useful to diagnose specifically where complexity is having an impact. Calculate Sales/SKU, Sales/Head Count, and Sales/Customer. If these are relatively low, chances are complexity is high—and vice versa. Some of these statistics are benchmarked in various publications, and that data can be a useful basis for comparison.

Where the complexity problems are much more involved, such as the minivan wiring-harness example described earlier, it is important to draw on more sophisticated solutions like those Emcien offers. Computers using the right algorithms can optimize even the most complex of situations. And now you know such tools are available.

Unmeasured = Unmanaged

What gets measured gets managed. The new metrics presented throughout this book help managers understand the likely consequences of their decisions and actions *before* they decide and take action. The true test of managers occurs when they understand how to quantify the likely outcome of decisions prior to making them. Once managers can evaluate what the likely outcome will be, there are alternative decisions that can be considered, and in the case of complexity, those alternatives might avoid some of the complexity-driven problems. There is even a chance that a decision can be made to avoid the complexity entirely.

War on Complexity

Earlier I described how Theresa Metty and her colleagues at Motorola waged war on complexity and succeeded. The major initiatives from that war were:

- Standardization, modularization, mass-customization, postponement
- Platforms and options: use managed variety
- Somebody has to discontinue the losers and dispose of the leftovers
- Gatekeepers are needed and they need rules to guide them
- Prioritize: If you try to be everything to everyone, you may end up being nothing to anyone

Once you have put the fundamental conditions in place, then enforcement of the rules becomes critical. Motorola used its Complexity Index. You may choose to develop one, or you might opt for some simpler, more immediate rules like these:

- Limit customers—fire the losers
- Limit SKUs—if you add one, drop one
- Limit suppliers—partner with the best, lose the rest
- Limit locations, markets, geography
- Redesign processes; use technology
- Selectively outsource what's context and keep what's core

A Side Effect of Outsourcing—Excess Capacity

A common question that arises shortly after a company begins outsourcing to faraway sources is, "What about our excess capacity?" As work moves out of existing plants, the overhead cost of the facility and its staff seldom goes down as fast as the volume of work. This means that the remaining work becomes more costly, as the remaining overhead is spread over a lower volume. This is a dangerous and potentially fatal trap. How do you get ahead of the curve and bring down fixed costs fast enough to allow the existing facility to compete on reduced volume?

First of all, if a large amount of work has moved out and the fixed costs are high and relatively difficult to lower, the facility may be doomed. The first outsourcing move, if a large one, may predetermine future moves. If the first move is a modest one—the more common case—it is imperative to move quickly and cut fixed overhead hard. This may mean selling or leasing part of the physical facility, selling some of the excess equipment, and certainly means cutting staff commensurate with the decline in work.

One of the complexities of outsourcing is that support-staff needs change very rapidly. The current support staff suddenly becomes too large, and the nature of the jobs associated with the outsourcing may not align with the skill sets of the current staff. The new jobs involve supplier support, liaison, quality assurance, logistics, and all involve heavy travel to the (often faraway) outsource location. Some may require physical relocation of people to the outsource country, or alternatively, hiring locally to support the outsourcing effort. Regardless of which path is followed, there is no time to waste. Action must be well thought out, but it must also be decisive, rapid, and proportional to the volume change. To do any less will be to accelerate the existing facility's demise.

A second complexity of outsourcing and the requisite cuts in fixed staffing is that some of the people that are cut have legacy knowledge that is important and valuable. In the case of large, (forced) early retirement programs, the loss of this legacy knowledge is often evident only after the fact, when problems that had once been solved reoccur, but the knowledge to solve them no longer resides in the organization. Outsourcing seems so simple on the surface—just buy instead of make—but it has its own set of complexities, which are usually underestimated. Consider such matters carefully before acting.

CONCLUSION

What Will You Do Differently, and Better?

"Whatever you can do, or dream you can, begin it.
Boldness has genius, power, and magic in it."
—Johann Wolfgang von Goethe, German poet, author,
and philosopher

Sometimes the hardest thing to do is to get started. The next hardest is to decide what to get started doing. Don't get hung up on this and let it paralyze you into inaction. Think about what you know, what you have already learned, and what you have read in the pages that precede this. Choose something to start on that is big enough to make a difference, and small enough to be manageable while you are getting the feel of it. Think big, but try small, then adjust based on what you learned and get going.

Don't let complexity slow you down. Complexity tends to create confusion and to make prioritization more difficult. As we discussed in Chapter 17, a specific framework for thought helps clarify what is important. The five elements any business needs to consider carefully are:

- Purpose
- Structure
- Processes
- Culture
- Relationships

As you try to manage complexity, there is another essential concept you must take into account: Value. Value is the ultimate metric of the twenty-first century, and whoever can create and deliver the best value wins.

The Shape of Value™

Value is a word that describes a combination of attributes and their consequences that meet higher-order needs of the customer. If we accept that value can be defined by just five large attributes, it can become the basis for part of the shared vision that all leaders must create.

THE ATTRIBUTES OF VALUE

- Quality
- Service
- Speed
- Cost
- Innovation

The right combination of these five attributes, each taken in a larger context, can define value and unify an organization in creating and consistently delivering that value. Complexity confuses value. It is a proverbial red herring, distracting an organization from its true goal, which is to obtain and keep a customer happy and satisfied. The organization can use many devices to drive out complexity and clarify the confusion it creates. The best choice of what to use is to focus on the wishes and needs of the customer—to be outside-in oriented—and those are best expressed in terms of value.

The Shape of Value™ Plot

In nearly every competitive situation, the best value wins. The figure below shows a simple polar graphic device I developed for my book *The Shape Shifters*. I call it the Shape of Value™ diagram. It depicts the relative shape of value of two well-known wristwatches: a Rolex and a Timex.

The Shape of Value Plot

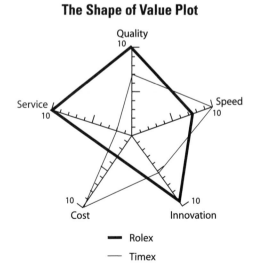

Imagine that each of the five axes is graduated from 0 to 10, from the center outward. Zero represents very low levels of each attribute labeled on the axis and 10 represents very high levels. Plot the relative "value rating" for each attribute, first for the Rolex, and then, using a different symbol, for the Timex. Then "connect the dots." The resulting shape is the shape of value for that watch. A group can debate and reach consensus on each point's placement, and the discussion/debate is part of the reason for the diagram—to come to a meeting of the minds—a shared vision about what represents value in this instance.

The example is so clear and simple, you will understand it as soon as you study it for a moment. Notice that the shape of value points toward the primary-purchase motivation. For the Rolex it is "innovation" or perhaps elements of the big definition of innovation, such as cachet, prestige, fashion, or style. For the Timex it is cost—or at least reliable timekeeping for a modest cost. This diagram can be used for any kind of product or service. Draw the five-axis Shape of Value stick figure and try one for yourself, comparing a bus versus a taxi versus a limousine service. The Shape of Value will also work to define the value perceptions of different consumers, retailers, buyers, etc. Try doing your own for a time-starved working single parent versus a well-to-do baby boomer, or alternatively, plot the differences between a Nordstrom shopper versus a Wal-Mart shopper.

Shape of the Business™

Each of the points listed under the framework for thought—Purpose, Structure, Processes, Culture, and Relationships—can also be placed on this five-axis polar diagram (just like the Shape of Value diagram uses) and used to depict the competitive differences between companies, the wishes of customers, etc. The relative positions of companies on the five dimensions of the Shape of the Business™—Purpose, Structure, Processes, Culture, and Relationships—can be used to draw competitive comparisons and to project the likely Shape of Value each might provide. Each of these dimensions of the Shape of the Business™ are instrumental in delivering one or more of the value attributes on the Shape of Value™ diagram. All of these uses are intended to reduce complexity by improving an organization's clarity of focus, and ultimately to help make decisions on whether to drive complexity out (lose it) or capitalize and compete on it (use it.)

These are powerful strategic and tactical tools, and that is what avoiding the Complexity Crisis is all about—knowing about and using such tools. Complexity is created in a business because of a lack of clarity of focus, and a desperate drive for growth and competitive advantage where it is hard or impossible to achieve. Since competitive advantage is all about having the best value, using the Shape of Value clarifies the focus on which value attributes will most likely lead to competitive success. Wasteful complexity is incurred when this focus is not clear. Valuable resources are wasted on work that does not create value from the perspective of the customer. Similarly, the company's structure, processes, culture, and relationships must be focused on doing those things that will create the right kind of value. Too often there are misguided initiatives that add little or no value, but create significant complexity.

Understand the relationship between the Shape of Value and the Shape of the Business. Then use tools such as these, combined with the solutions described previously, to minimize complexity—to find it, drive it out, and keep it out (or, if the value is right, choose to compete on complexity).

To Know, to Care, to Struggle, and to Do It with Passion

Earlier I listed four formulas to describe "knowing." I want to repeat them here, but add a fifth one.

1. Data + Organization = Information
2. Information + Insight = Knowledge
3. Knowledge + Experience = Wisdom
4. Wisdom + Imagination = Genius

These four formulas lead to a final, fifth formula:

5. Good People + Good Partners + Strong Leadership + Appropriate Technology = Competitive Success

Working in unison with partners, with a focus on the purpose and goals of the organization, is essential.

The Call to Action

The final question for you, as a manager or leader, is "What will you do differently because of the new knowledge you have gained?" Knowledge alone is not enough. It must be combined with experience and insights and then it is only effective if you take action on your decisions. Find the places where complexity has crippled your company and drive it out. Share your newfound knowledge with others in your organization so that you can help one another to be successful. Enlist others in the effort. Plan, analyze, and then make decisions; above all, take action on those decisions. The decision to begin is the most important step in conquering complexity. The action you take based on that decision is what will lead to success. Start now!

WORKS QUOTED AND CITED

Carbone, James. "Motorola Leverages Its Way to Lower Cost," Online, 16 September 2004.

Carbone, Jim. "Motorola Simplifies to Lower Cost," *Purchasing Magazine,* 18 October 2001.

The George Group. Special Report: "Unraveling Complexity in Products and Services," Knowledge@Wharton, *http://knowledge .wharton.upenn.edu.*

George, Michael L., and Stephen A. Wilson. *Conquering Complexity in Your Business* (New York: McGraw-Hill, 2004).

Gottfredson, Mark, and Keith Aspinall. "Innovation vs. Complexity—What Is too Much of a Good Thing?" *Harvard Business Review,* November 2005, pp. 62–71.

Handfield, Rob. "Managing Complexity in the Supply Chain: Motorola's War on Supply Chain Complexity," *Supply Chain Management Review,* 7 July 2004.

Kadlec, Bill. "Full Life-Cycle SKU Rationalization For Retail." Acorn Systems, Sept. 2005, *www.acornsys.com.*

Kauffman, Stuart A. *The Origins of Order* (Oxford: Oxford University Press, 1993).

Levitt, Theodore. "Creativity Is Not Enough," *Harvard Business Review Classic,* August 2002.

Lewin, Roger. *Complexity: Life at the Edge of Chaos* (New York: Collier Books, 1992).

Maier, Matthew. "A Radical Fix for Airlines: Make Flying Free," *Business* 2.0, April 2006.

Mariotti, John L. *Making Partnerships Work* (Oxford, UK: Capstone/Wiley, 2002).

Mariotti, John L. *The Power of Partnerships* (Cambridge, MA: Blackwell, 1995).

Mariotti, John L. "Selling More for Less," *Management Centre Europe Trend Tracker,* 2Q, 2003.

Mariotti, John L. *The Shape Shifters* (Hoboken, NJ: Wiley 1997).

Mariotti, John L. *Smart Things to Know about Partnerships* (Oxford, UK: Capstone/Wiley, 2001).

Mariotti, John L. "Too Much 'Tech Talk'—Not Enough 'Trust Talk,'" *Supply Chain Management Review,* 1998: Second Quarter issue.

Metty, Theresa. Chief Procurement Officer, Motorola, Inc., speech presentation and private conversations, 2003.

Moore, Geoffrey. *Inside the Tornado* (New York: Harper Business, 1995); other books include *Crossing the Chasm* and *Gorilla Game.*

Pagels, Heinz R. *The Dreams of Reason* (New York: Bantam Books, 1989).

Pine, B. Joseph II. *Mass Customization* (Boston: Harvard Business School Press, 1993).

Ries, Al, and Jack Trout. *Positioning—The Battle for Your Mind* (New York: McGraw-Hill, 1981).

Schwartz, Barry. *The Paradox of Choice—Why More Is Less* (New York: Harper Collins, 2004).

Selden, Larry, and Geoffrey Colvin. *Angel Customers and Demon Customers* (New York: Portfolio Imprint, Penguin Group, 2003).

White, Cherish. "Motorola's Battle with Supply and Demand Chain Complexity," *Supply and Demand Chain Executive and iSource Business,* April/May 2003.

INDEX